Working with your Dentist

...and helping with family dental care

Working with your Dentist

Maurice Hart and
Andrew McWilliam

Quiller Press
London

ISBN 1 899163 14 X

First published 1996 by:
Quiller Press Limited
46 Lillie Road
London SW6 1TN

Designed by Jo Lee
Printed and bound in Great Britain by
Biddles Ltd, Guildford and King's Lynn

Contents

Acknowledgements

The authors would like to thank all those who have been involved with the production and publication of this book. We would also like to thank the many people who have helped with ideas, suggestions for content and useful criticisms.

We are especially grateful to:

Margaret, Caroline and Angela McWilliam for their help and patience during the writing of the book.

Denplan for allowing the use of the picture on the front cover, for making constructive comments on particular sections of the book, and their support for the production and use of the book.

Frazer Wanstall BDS for giving careful advice on dental problems which helped with the initial concept of producing such a book.

Marion Carey for her helpful advice on the position with regard to library health books and for encouraging us at an early stage in the writing of the book.

We are also grateful for permission to use:

Four diagrams taken from the book 'Textbook for Dental Nurses' written by H.Levison and published by Blackwell Scientific.

One diagram taken from the book 'Endodontics in Clinical Practice' written by F.J.Hardy and published by Wright.

Chapter 1

Introduction

what the book is about,
layout of the chapters

This is a family dental reference book. It provides guidance for people of all ages on how to stay in good dental health for their lifetime by working closely with their dentist and by taking good personal dental care. The authors have set out to give as much help and support to dental patients as possible. The content of the book and the arrangement of the chapters have been carefully designed to make the book fully informative but also interesting and easy for readers to use.

A major purpose of the book is to enable readers to follow up explanations and information given to them by their dentist. It can be difficult for dental patients to concentrate on a dentist's explanations when they are sitting in the treatment chair. Patients may also not think of follow-up questions or find it difficult to ask them. This communication problem often occurs when people feel under pressure, particularly when they may also be suffering from trauma after injections and other treatments. When readers use this book to follow up a dentist's explanations they will be able to investigate the nature of their dental problems and the treatments suggested for such problems in their own homes and in their own time. The use of the book in this way will also help the dentist, as it will reduce the need to try to make every detail and all the options for treatment clear during the fixed time available for treating the person concerned. This follow-up activity is likely to be especially helpful when there is a possible choice of treatment. The book will then supply readers with details that will enable them to have an informed discussion with their dentist about such choices.

This is the first book to be published that gives relatively detailed information on a very wide range of dental care to the general public. The book is a part of the new trend in medicine of trying to involve patients more in their own health care generally, and in decision making about treatments in particular. By using this book, readers will acquire a greater knowledge of dental matters and will consequently be able to help themselves and their children by being more aware of the possibilities. They will also feel more in control of their own dental state and appearance. A greater awareness by patients will also help the dentist, because more knowledge will nearly always result in a more relaxed patient. It is the tension in patients that is very often the most troublesome aspect of treatment for dentists.

Everybody should have healthy and good-looking teeth and gums, or efficient and good-looking replacements for lost teeth. A major objective for this book is to help readers keep in that state for their lifetime. Some problems with teeth and gums are unavoidable, and some aspects of the care of teeth and gums need professional care, so working closely with a dentist is essential. On the other hand, it is important to realise that the frequency and severity of dental problems can often be reduced considerably by a change in dietary habits and improved personal oral care. The information given in this book will help readers to understand why the role of diet and self care are vital to dental health both for themselves and for their children.

Another feature of the book is that any information a reader might want to know about dental matters is available, from teeth and gums and their day-to-day care, dental first aid in the home to what to expect for different age ranges. Readers with families can also use the book to find information on preventing accidental damage, choosing between NHS and private treatment, the choice of different forms of dental insurance, and possible careers in dentistry for young people. The book is also about people, as the case studies describe the problems, treatments, and reactions of particular individuals. The case studies provide a human interest that may be useful in family discussions.

The layout of the chapters in the book

The chapters in this book have been arranged in a way that is designed to help readers to find their way around easily and to be able to start reading at places that are relevant to them. A common way of using the book will be after a visit to the dentist when a problem like the need for root canal filling or an extraction has been identified. In such cases the chapter headings or the index will lead the reader directly to relevant sections. Other readers who may just have purchased the book, or who are looking for more general information, may well want to use the book in other ways. The main purpose of this section on the layout is to indicate what other ways of using the book have been built into the arrangement of the chapters.

An important feature of the design of the book is that it has three distinct parts. The first five chapters form the first part and can be considered as an extended introduction. This first part of the book gives information in general terms rather than in precise detail. Chapters 2 to 5 provide different ways into the book: by the age of a person (Chapter 2), by a reason for a visit to a dentist (Chapter 3), by looking for answers to questions (Chapter 4), or by comparison with other peoples experiences (Chapter 5). All of these chapters contain references to later chapter for readers who want more information. First-time readers will probably want to start by comparing their own dental state with the relevant age group in Chapter 2. After that they might find it helpful to read either Chapter 4 or Chapter 5, as these two chapters provide some human interest and will give an early indication of how useful the book can be when people have dental problems.

Chapters 6 to 16 form the middle part of the book. It is here that specific information is given about dental problems and possible treatments for those problems. Chapters 6, 7 and 8 act as an introduction to this part. These three chapters give explanations and information about the make up of teeth, the records dentists keep, and the nature of the patient experience during dental treatment. These details then apply to all the treatments described subsequently. New readers might find it helpful to look through Chapters 6, 7 and 8 soon after acquiring the book.

Chapters 6 to 13 look different to the rest of the book because they give explanations and information at two levels. These chapters start with a summary level that has the heading **'Summary level'** and which is printed on a grey background. Each chapter then continues with a more detailed level that is headed **'Detailed level'** and which is printed as normal on a white background. The difference between the two levels is indicated in this way so that a reader need only go on to the more detailed level if they think it necessary for a deeper understanding. The deeper level normally contains a description of individual problems, possible treatments for these problems and what these treatments entail in terms of time, procedures and costs. This deeper level will also give implications for future health and appearance where relevant.

Chapters 14, 15, and 16 are also in the middle part of the book. These chapters discuss a wide range of problems and treatments, but all at one level. Chapter 14 deals with accidental damage. Chapter 15 deals with many different problems, most occurring only rarely and some needing referral to specialists rather than treatment at a general dental practice. The newer treatments described in Chapter 16 will be of interest to many, particularly the new possibilities for much less traumatic alternatives to injections and fillings.

Chapters 17, 18, and 19 form the end part of the book. These chapters give other information on matters relating to dentistry that are of interest to individuals, families and teachers. These include details of home dental first aid, the choice between NHS and private treatment, the choice of different insurance schemes, where to obtain further information, and possible careers for young people in dentistry.

As another aid for the reader the diagrams or figures used in the book are labelled for easy cross reference, so that Figure 6.3 is the third figure in Chapter 6.

How the book helps when there are options for treatment

It is certainly true that most people become deeply concerned about dental problems at some stage in their lives. This concern can spring from symptoms such as severe pain followed by an abscess, teeth becoming loose, sore and bleeding gums and for teenagers misaligned teeth. When such problems occur difficult decisions often have to be made by the patient and dentist in consultation. Typical examples of these options are: what type of filling material is to be used, whether to treat or extract a tooth that is causing an abscess, whether to use a bridge or a denture to replace missing teeth and what kind of treatment to use for misaligned teeth. Such choices can affect future health and appearance and given that a complex dental bridge can cost more than £3000, the decisions often have considerable financial implications. A large part of the book is devoted to giving details about dental problems and the choice of treatments available from dentists. It is when there are options like those given above that the book will be especially helpful. In such cases readers will be able to read about treatments at a deeper level if they wish. They are also likely to find that a question in Chapter 4 or a case study in Chapter 5 is relevant and so will give another useful comparison for their situation.

Chapter 2

Family Considerations

expectations for age ranges

This chapter is placed at the beginning of the book for two reasons. The first reason is to emphasise the fact that this is a family dental reference book by noting how family considerations can be very important for dental care. The second reason is that the expectations for age ranges given in this chapter provide a good starting point for using the book, especially for new readers. A reader can look up the expectations for their own age range and for any other age range in which they have an interest. It will then be possible to make a comparison with the dental health of everyone concerned. References to other parts of the book are then given in the details for each age range.

Family considerations

The book is designed to be placed with other reference books on a family bookshelf and it is hoped that children will be encouraged to read it. If visiting the dentist is seen as a part of family life, with dental problems and possible treatments discussed within the family, then the use of this book will help to make such discussions much more meaningful.

An important part of being a parent must be to find out as much as possible about what is needed to give their children a good start to a healthy life. This is especially true of dental care. The relevant sections in this chapter give details of tooth development in babies and young children, and the causes of and treatments for possible problems.

In general terms children need to be encouraged by their parents to visit the dentist, to follow a sensible diet, and to practise good dental hygiene. An extreme example of what can happen if a mother is not aware of the correct dental care for her baby is given in Case Study 1 in Chapter 5. As another example of the need for parental direction, around 3% of all young people between the ages of 11 and 24 loose teeth through advanced gum disease. This disease is nearly always caused by neglect. Case Study 7 in Chapter 5 is an illustration of the results of such neglect. If advanced gum disease occurs in a young person, it almost certainly means they clean their teeth inefficiently and/or very rarely; they will also not have visited a dentist on a regular basis.

If losing teeth through such neglect is due to parents not encouraging good dental care, then it would be a very sad outcome for the young person concerned.

Dentists sometimes find that parents are worried that their children are not keeping up in terms of tooth development. The development of teeth and the range of problems that occur are like all other human conditions in that there is a very wide range of possibilities. For example the 0-3 years section of this chapter notes that babies are usually born without teeth, but in 1990, Shaun Keaney of Newbury was born with twelve teeth. Parents should therefore not worry unduly if young children are not conforming exactly to the norm in terms of development. On the other hand it is important to monitor development and to seek the advice of professionals if there are concerns.

One particular time when family support can be crucial is when a teenager needs orthodontic treatment for misaligned teeth. This problem is discussed in some detail in the Age 11-15 section of this chapter. As a part of orthodontic treatment the teenager concerned may have to wear a rather ugly appliance on their teeth for up to two years, and this gives an indication of the problems that can arise and why family support is so vitally important. The fact that three of the case studies in Chapter 5 are about orthodontic treatment emphasises this importance.

The importance of family support in dental matters is not of course limited to just parents looking after their children. Support, discussion and encouragement are helpful between any family members, or indeed between friends. One group who do often need support more than others are the elderly. It is very easy for both older people and their families to assume that no more can be done in terms of dental care. Such an assumption is very far from being true, as described in both the Age 45-64, and the Age 65 and over sections in this chapter and as illustrated by Case Study 12 in Chapter 5.

It should be noted that NHS dental treatment is free for those under 18, so it is worth trying to find a dentist who will treat young people under NHS dental provision, even if adults have to pay privately. Older people whose only income is the state pension may also qualify for free or nearly free treatment.

Expectations for age ranges

In 1978 about one third of the adult population of the UK had no natural teeth. By 1994 that figure had improved to only one fifth. This change happened largely because of better dental care and improved personal dental hygiene. Also important were improvements in dental treatment technology, increased knowledge about the causes of problems and changing attitudes to the use of extraction as a first option in many cases. Given proper care, natural teeth should normally be retained for a lifetime and this book is seen as a contributing factor to achieving that end. The purpose of this part of this chapter is to give readers an indication of what the main considerations might be at various stages of their life.

As people move through their lives, their teeth and gums are subject to natural physical changes. Problems can also be caused by wear and the nature of dental care. In this chapter the population is divided into eight groups starting at 'Age 0-3' and ending at '65 and over'. Within each group details are given of physical changes, notes on common problems and actions that should be taken for different ages. Cross-references to relevant case studies in Chapter 5 are given for age groups where relevant. Parents can check on what to expect for their children and then work with them to ensure proper dental care and adults can compare the condition of their own teeth and mouths with the expectation for the appropriate age range as given here.

The rest of this chapter discusses concerns for particular age groups divided into eight groups as follows:

Age 0-3   Age 4-6   Age 7-10   Age 11-15   Age 16-25
Age 26-45   Age 46-64   Age 65 and over

Age 0-3

Figure 2.1 is a pictorial representation of a full lower set of deciduous teeth. These teeth are also known as milk or temporary teeth. The upper set is a near mirror image of the lower set so that there are twenty teeth in a full set of deciduous teeth.

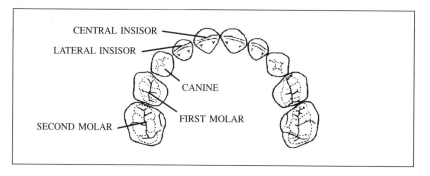

Figure 2.1

One of the major concerns with babies is 'teething'. Technically the appearance of the deciduous teeth through the gums is known as eruption. Deciduous teeth start developing before birth, but normally do not start to erupt until after about six months.

Lower teeth tend to appear before upper teeth and average ages of eruption are as follows:

Central incisors	6 months	Canines	18 months
Lateral incisors	8 months	Second molars	24 months
First molars	12 months		

As permanent teeth do not normally start to erupt until the age of six or seven, the deciduous teeth have to function effectively as a part of the first stage of the digestive system for six or seven years. Deciduous teeth have the same basic structure as permanent teeth (as described in Chapter 6) and can suffer from the tooth disease caries and the gum disease gingivitis. While it is possible to fill deciduous teeth, it is very beneficial to tooth and mouth development if fillings are not necessary. Eruption (teething) can be painful and cause discomfort. Teething also seems to interact with infections in the same way that adults find that colds etc generate toothache occasionally.

Accidental damage to teeth occurs in about one in twelve children before they reach the age of five. Such damage is most likely to happen at the toddler stage. This damage is usually easily rectified, but does need action as soon as possible. If the damage is severe, such as a tooth being loose or broken off, then the child should be treated immediately. Accidental damage is dealt with in detail in Chapter 14 and if an accident does occur at home, the section on dental first aid in Chapter 17 will provide advice on any immediate action that should be taken.

Suggestions for the dental care for this age group follow clearly from the knowledge of how caries and gingivitis develop that will be established in Chapter 6 and the notes about dental treatment in Chapter 3. People with babies might find it particularly useful to read the part of Chapter 6 that describes how caries develops. They will then see why it is particularly important to guard this age group against caries by strictly limiting the intake of foods or drinks that contain sugar. In some families it becomes a habit to use sweets as a reward and/or sweets, sweet drinks or a dummy dipped in a sweet substance as a way of pacifying a crying or upset baby. There will be two major effects if this procedure is followed. The first is that the child is likely to start developing the disease caries very quickly (Case Study 1 in Chapter 5 vividly illustrates this problem). The second and equally important effect is that a habit developed at this age is likely to be a habit that lasts a lifetime. The adult who habitually uses sweet things for comfort is likely to have a lifetime of dental problems with a consequent effect on appearance and expense.

This is also an appropriate time to mention the value of fluoride. It has been scientifically shown that, if fluoride is present when teeth are formed, then such teeth are much more resistant to caries attack. If the water supply is not treated with fluoride, then a toothpaste with fluoride, or treatment using commercially available fluoride additives is a must for this age group.

Making baby a part of the family for dental care is another guard against caries and the major factor in the prevention of gingivitis. Babies should have a toothbrush and clean their teeth like their parents and any brothers and sisters.

This cleaning is not going to be effective for some years, but it is the habit that is important. As soon as teeth appear they need to be cleaned on a regular, twice a day basis, probably with toothpaste on a clean damp piece of gauze initially. Babies should also visit the dentist with other members of the family in order to make sure that development is proceeding properly and in order to feel that going to the dentist is a natural family activity and nothing frightening or unusual. If the child is registered as an NHS patient then the dentist will receive a fee for caring for this child patient.

Age 4-6

In some ways this is a fairly stable time for dental progression. Permanent teeth will be forming and the first permanent molars (see Figure 7.2) can appear before a child's seventh birthday. In general, however, the major dental concern for this age group is the care of their set of deciduous teeth. The make-up of teeth is described in Chapter 6. Deciduous teeth are similar to permanent teeth in most respects (see Figure 6.1) but also have some differences. The enamel on the crown of the teeth is much thinner and the pulp chamber is relatively large. The fact that the enamel is thinner means that caries attack can reach the dentine more quickly.

At the present time about one in five of this age group have to be treated for caries attack with fillings or extractions. Parents need to be aware of a possible caries attack, with even the possibility of an abscess on the gum, by noting if children have toothache, pain with hot and cold food, red and swollen gums etc. If fillings are necessary then reading Chapter 9 and making the child aware of some of the nature of treatment for fillings would also be helpful. Accidental damage is also quite common for this age group. Accidental damage is dealt with in detail in Chapter 14 and if an accident does occur at home, the section on dental first aid in Chapter 17 will provide advice on any immediate action that should be taken.

Deciduous teeth tend to be whiter than permanent teeth. The roots of the back teeth are more spread out than their permanent replacements in order to leave a space for the development of the crowns of the permanent teeth. The deciduous teeth are also obviously smaller than their permanent successors. At this age, it is possible for dentists to be able to make judgements about possible problems with the placing and size of the prospective permanent teeth. These are problems that need orthodontic management (as described in Chapter 13), which is always best administered as soon as possible.

By using the details given in Chapter 6 of this book, it should also be possible to alert a child of this age to the dental 'story'. How plaque builds up, how sugar reacts with saliva to form acid and attack the enamel, how the pulp at the centre of each tooth performs a hurting and mending function similar to the blood that appears when they scrape their knee. The use of plaque discloser on the child's teeth will give the story a practical element. All of this kind of activity can involve the child in the teeth-cleaning process and alert the boy or girl to the dangers involved in a heavy intake of sweet things. There are also many leaflets and booklets especially produced to encourage good dental habits for children. Such literature may be distributed at school or given to children by a dentist. Much of this material can also be obtained from other local and national sources as noted in Chapter 17.

It is also vital for this age group that they have a regular visit to the dentist. During such visits the dentist will try to ensure that deciduous teeth do not have to be extracted. Orthodontic problems can be diagnosed and solutions suggested at an early stage. Any necessary scaling and polishing can be done. Dentists will also emphasise to this age group how important it is to look after teeth and so can be seen to reinforce the dental 'story' suggested in the previous paragraph.

When children start school they may be seen by a school dentist at intervals throughout their school careers. Case Study 1 in Chapter 5 concerns a boy in this age group.

Age 7-10

Children in this age group all undergo a period of radical change in their dental development. During this time most of the deciduous teeth will be replaced by permanent teeth. This process generally starts with the first permanent molars erupting at the back of the deciduous teeth which may happen before the child is seven. These are the four teeth given the number 6 on a dental chart (see Figures 7.1 and 7.2). In general, the deciduous teeth are then replaced by permanent teeth starting from the front. This process is not normally complete until the young person has reached the age of 11 or 12. There are two biological features which it is helpful for children to understand as they start on this process.

The first biological feature is the way that the replacement process happens.The roots of deciduous teeth start to be re-absorbed, under the influence of the permanent teeth beneath, about 2 or 3 years before the tooth is lost. When this process of re-absorption is complete and deciduous teeth are ready for replacement, they have no roots and become loose. Actually removing deciduous teeth has a history of different methods and consequences. If a deciduous tooth can be removed naturally by the child then that is fine, but dentists will effect the removal if required. Many parents still use the services of the 'tooth fairy' who wants baby teeth and is prepared to pay £1 for them! When this page was being written the Xmas copy of Radio Times pictured a child with the two top front teeth missing and the song 'All I want for Christmas is my two front teeth' is still a best-seller. The occasion of permanent teeth replacing deciduous teeth is an important marker in a child's progression to being grown up and it is probably right to mark the fact with some ceremony. It is also of course a useful time to emphasise how important it is to look after permanent teeth.

The second biological feature is that most replacement permanent teeth are not fully formed when they appear. Only around two thirds of their root length has formed when they erupt. In particular, looking at Figure 6.1 and reading the detail given with this diagram, the apical foramen is left as a relatively large gap. It takes about three years for the roots to grow to their full length and the apical foramen to close. This feature leaves the permanent teeth in question rather more susceptible to accidental damage, but also means that if damage does occur then healing is more likely than in adults.

Because this is a period of radical dental change it is important for parents and the family dentist to monitor progress. Problems occur frequently and then need action by a dentist in order to keep effects to a minimum. During this period the child is also likely to be seen by a dentist at school, as a part of the national community dental care programme. Any problems identified here will be referred to parents. Some of the more common of these problems will be described next.

In general, permanent teeth erupt using deciduous teeth as position markers. This means that if any deciduous teeth have been lost, then particular care and observation is needed. Occasionally permanent teeth start to erupt while deciduous teeth are still in place, usually then either in front of or behind the existing deciduous teeth. Another common problem is that people can have permanent teeth that are too large for a small jaw, so that there is not enough room for all the permanent teeth. All of these problems come under the heading

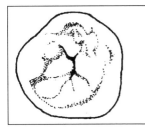

Figure 2.2

of 'orthodontic treatment' and are described in more detail in Chapter 13. About one half of all young people need some kind of orthodontic treatment. Case Study 2 in Chapter 5 is relevant here even though that young person's age was 11.

One other feature which might need treatment is indicated by Figure 2.2, which is a pictorial representation of the top of the crown of a typical back tooth.

Another way of describing Figure 2.2 is that it shows the occlusal (or chewing) surface of a typical back tooth. The occlusal surfaces of back teeth are not completely smooth; they have crevices and if these crevices are particularly deep they can become a site for plaque accumulation and consequent caries attack. Such deeper crevices are known as fissures. Fissures can be made less deep in order to guard against plaque accumulation. This process is known as **fissure sealing** and is similar to fillings as dealt with in detail in Chapter 9. If fissure sealing is needed then it should be done as soon as a back tooth is fully formed after eruption.

Children in this age group are at the stage where they are growing up very rapidly. They are also usually becoming very aware of their appearance. As with every other age group, too much sugar intake and lack of proper cleaning can soon lead to attacks of caries. The necessity of close monitoring of permanent teeth eruption makes regular visits to the dentist an even more necessary part of life for this age group. Accidental damage is again relevant for this group. This consideration is particularly appropriate if the child is keen on games that involve the use of a hard ball, when the use of a flexible gum shield might be sensible. The prevention and treatment for accidental damage is dealt with in detail in Chapter 14, and if an accident does occur at home, the section on dental first aid in Chapter 17 will provide advice on any immediate action that should be taken.

As with the 4-6 age group, it is important to encourage children of this age group to learn about the dental 'story', including the structure of teeth and gums, what causes them problems, and how to avoid such problems. The educational materials mentioned in the section for the 4-6 age group are equally relevant for this age group.

Age 11-15

During the early part of this period it is likely that the four molars second from the back will erupt (see Figure 7.2). This period is also the time when any major necessary orthodontic work needs to be done and the sight of young teenagers with braces on their teeth is very familiar.

Caries attack and gingivitis are quite common for this age group and so there is often a need for periodontal treatment (seen Chapter 12). Virtually all of this age group will need some kind of remedial dental treatment at some time. This can also be the time when teenagers start to rebel against previous disciplines and habits that parents have tried to establish and this rebellion can work against proper care of teeth among all the other issues like bed times, staying out late and spending money on clothes. Investigations have shown that only around half of this age group attend a dentist for regular check-ups. Appearance is rated very highly in this age group so they need to realise that missing teeth and diseased gums or teeth do not look very pretty. Maybe even worse is the fact that a major symptom of gingivitis is bad breath. It is undeniable that looking good and being attractive has to include good dental habits.

Accidental damage is very much more possible for this group if they are involved in sport. Physical contact becomes harder and in ball games the ball is likely to be travelling at greater speeds than for younger age groups. The use of a gum shield is strongly recommended. The provision of gum shields is described in detail in Chapter 14 and if an accident does occur at home, the section on dental first aid in Chapter 17 will provide advice on any immediate action that should be taken. Case Study 3 in Chapter 5 discusses the results of accidental damage.

Given the common dental problems that beset this age group then Chapters 9, 13 and 14 are particularly relevant for them. The book supplies information that should help young people of this age group to acquire a mature attitude towards dental care. If the family dentist starts to treat the young person more like an adult that can also be helpful in encouraging them to be more responsible in the area of dental care. Because of the vital importance of involving members of this age group in decision-making, particularly for orthodontic treatment, there are four case studies devoted to this age group (2,3,4 and 5 in Chapter 5).

Age 16-25

The only major dental change for this age group is that the so-called wisdom teeth erupt (the four teeth numbered 8 in Figure 7.1). There can be considerable problems with these particular teeth. They often grow in strange directions and have unusual root systems, so it is important for this age group to realise that there could be potential difficulties. Along with the 11-16 age group this is the time of life when caries attack is most common. Even at this age, total neglect can soon lead to tooth loss. Replacements for teeth in the form of bridges or dentures can be expensive. In some parts of the UK there are reports of unemployed people of this age having to live with unfilled gaps in their teeth.

There are other factors that can affect different sections of this age group. One of these factors is pregnancy. There can be a considerable deterioration in teeth of pregnant women, so regular frequent visits to the dentist should be a priority as soon as pregnancy is confirmed. The reality of such potential problems is confirmed by the fact that NHS dental treatment for pregnant women is free. The possibility of accidental damage during sport is even more possible than for the 11-16 age group. The use of a gum shield is again strongly recommended. Another possibility for this age group is cosmetic dental treatment. This can be different from orthodontics in that it can sometimes involve fairly drastic measures to alter the appearance of teeth and gums. Cosmetic treatment is not covered in detail in this book; it is likely to involve the use of specialist private treatment.

As with the 11-16 age group, virtually everybody in this age group will need some dental remedial action. Using this book to be informed of problems and possible remedies, both for themselves and new families, plus building a co-operative and ongoing relationship with a dentist are the best way for this age group to ensure their dental future. People in this group certainly need a regular six monthly pattern of visits to their dentist.

Case studies 6 and 7 in Chapter 5 concern people in this age group.

Age 26-45

There are no anatomical changes for this age group and any orthodontic treatment will almost certainly have been completed. If the teeth are well cared for there is less occurrence of caries attack in this age group, but if dental care has been neglected then this is the period when gingivitis is likely to turn to periodontitis (as described in Chapter 6) and treatment will be needed. The number of post 25-year-olds in the UK with gum disease at some level is over

80%. This seems a very large number of people, but it does include many who have gum disease problems at a very low level. Chapters 6 and 12 give the full details, but one conclusion that has to be drawn from this high percentage is the necessity for regular visits to the dentist to help to control this disease. As noted in the 16-25 group, pregnancy can have a considerable effect on the mother's teeth. Women who are pregnant should refer to that section.

This is a busy time for dental treatment as emphasised by the fact that at the age of 45 the average person has at least half of their teeth either filled or extracted. During this period people will often be thinking more about planning for the future in terms of pensions etc. and the same is certainly true for dental care. If there are any problems with individual teeth then dentists will do their utmost to avoid extraction, as the loss of the first tooth (unless it is a wisdom tooth) can be the first step on a fairly rapid downward path. Personal care needs to be seen in the same light; keeping healthy teeth and gums in these years is vital insurance for the future. Regular six-monthly visits to the dentist are an essential feature of this care.

Case Study 8 in Chapter 5 gives an account of the dental problems of someone who just fits in to the upper end of this age group. This case study is particularly important for this age group because it illustrates what can happen if there is a lack of consistent care during this age range. Such a situation can arise very easily because this is often such a busy time of life spent building up a career and caring for a young family.

Age 46-64

Problems for this age group often arise more frequently than for the 26-45 age group, partly because of the work that teeth and gums have had to do in the previous 45 years and also because of gradual changes that can eventually cause problems. In particular the gums slowly recede and the pulp chamber becomes smaller. This age group will probably have received many fillings and each of these can cause problems through wear and tear, or caries appearing underneath the filling. Caries can also occur where gums have receded.

The good news for this age group is that fewer people are losing all their teeth. If a person starts this period with no dentures and all teeth in a reasonably sound state and then looks after them well, with regular visits to the dentist, then they will almost certainly finish this period with at least a part of the same teeth in place. Why it may only be a 'part', is that some teeth might have needed to be crowned. Chapter 10 on root treatments and crowns is likely to be relevant for this age group.

Case studies 9, 10 and 11 in Chapter 5 concern people in this age group. One of these shows the result of neglect. The other two illustrate the fact that determined and knowledgeable members of this age group can have a considerable part to play in decision making in terms of their own dental health and appearance. This is especially the case if they are willing to pay for more expensive options.

Age 65 and over

It is realised that 65 and over is likely to cover a wider age range that any of the others in this chapter. In a way that is good news, because with the possibilities now available there is no reason why anybody, even up to a hundred or more years old, should not have an efficient and comfortable set of either natural teeth, or dentures, or a mixture of these and other possibilities. For many in this age group there will in fact be little difference in expectations from the 46-64 age group. Certainly anyone who is at the beginning of this time in their life should also refer to the 46-64 section. In particular Chapter 10 and Case Studies 9,10 and 11 in Chapter 5 are likely to be relevant for many in this age group.

Appearance and health for this age group are perhaps even more affected by dental factors than other age groups. The possibilities in terms of crowns, bridges, replacement teeth, dentures or various combinations of all of these are summarised in Chapter 11, and this chapter is likely to be especially relevant to this age group. The time of transition from mainly natural teeth to whole or partial dentures can be difficult. If the change is made too late the person concerned might not find it easy to adapt to the art of using dentures.

People in this age group reading this book will have realised the importance of the continuing care of natural teeth, including a sugar-free diet as far as possible. They will also realise the importance of continued regular visits to the dentist. These regular visits are still important even if the person has no natural teeth left. Another major emphasis of this chapter is on the family and readers who have elderly relatives, or who are carers, may sometimes need to overcome the idea that dental pain and discomfort is a natural part of getting old. In particular the fittings of dentures needs to be checked at least once a year.

Case study 12 in Chapter 5 concerns someone from this age group and is particularly relevant for families or others who have care of an elderly person. It may be also be useful for some members of this age group to note that, under the NHS, dentists can make home visits to the aged and infirm. It is likely that many members of this age group, especially those whose only income is the old age pension, will qualify for extra financial help for dental treatment under the NHS. The dentist or dental receptionist will supply the relevant forms and give details on how to apply for such payments.

Chapter 3

Going to the Dentist

reasons for visits and possible treatments

T his chapter is placed at this early position in the book in order to give another starting point for using the book. The table given in this chapter lists nine common reasons for visiting the dentist, and indicates the nature of the treatments which can be given during these visits. Also in the table are references to other relevant parts of the book. Readers can therefore check to see if visits they make to their dentist fit into one of the nine categories given in the table. The table will then give a quick guide on what the relevant treatments may be, plus references to the questions chapter, the case studies chapter and other chapters which relate to that category of visit.

There are three different kinds of reference given in the table. References in the first column are preceded either by the letter 'Q' or by the letters 'CS'. Q stands for question, so that 'Q3' refers to Question 3 in Chapter 4; while 'CS3' refers to Case Study 3 in Chapter 5. The numbers given in the second column in brackets refer to subsequent chapters that contain details of relevant treatments. Where there is more than one number, the first number gives the most relevant chapter; so that (10,6,8) means that Chapters 6,8 and 10 are all relevant to the problem and treatment, but Chapter 10 is the most directly relevant.

Note that all treatments referred to in this table are described in full in later chapters.

Initial or routine periodic visit	Teeth examination – question patient – Fill in or check on chart, make notes on diagnosis of problems (7)
	Possible scale and polish (12, 6)
	Possible X-rays for diagnosis (8)
	Arrange other appointments if necessary

Initial emergency visit	Question patient – teeth examination – Fill in or check on chart, make notes on diagnosis of problems (7) First priority to relieve pain (9) Possible X-rays for diagnosis (8) Arrange other appointments if necessary
Caries Fillings **Q1**	Caries causes cavities, pain may or may not be present If cavity not reached pulp – treatment is filling – involves removing diseased tissue replacing with filling compound – local anaesthetic by injection (9, 6, 8, 16) One or two fillings can be done in one visit
Caries Abscesses Root canal treatment **Q2 CS9**	If caries reaches pulp then pain and possible abscess – abscess has to cured first (6) Usual subsequent treatment by root canal filling – all pulp removed and replaced by compound, long and fairly difficult procedure – often needs anaesthetic by injection (10, 6, 8, 9) If crown still largely in place root filling completed by ordinary filling – but root filling often followed eventually by collapse of crown (10)
Crowns **Q2 CS8, 9, 10**	If the crown of a tooth has collapsed or is no longer viable then an artificial crown is used Some crowns have to be anchored on posts reaching down into the root canal as well as by adhesives, other crowns are attached to built up fillings strengthened by using pins (10) The procedure needs two or more visits. Crowns have to be made individually for each patient

Extractions Bridges Dentures Q2, 3, 4 CS1, 6, 8, 10, 11, 12	if teeth or their anchorage become non viable then teeth extracted as a last resort (11, 6) Lost teeth replaced by bridges or dentures (10) Will need a series of visits
Gingivitis Periodontal disease CS7	Problems with gums and supporting structures of teeth Prevention by regular visits – scaling and polishing Limited progression treated by removing tartar in enlarged gingival crevice – sometime needs anaesthetic Considerable progression of the disease may need minor oral surgery and/or extraction (12, 6, 15) Likely to need a series of visits – some treatment can be done by a trained dental hygienist
Orthodontics Q5 CS2, 4, 5	Dealing with misaligned teeth and poor occlusion Most usually carried out between 7-14 years (13) Needs treatment for a period of time up to 2 years
Other conditions CS3, 6	These can include accidental damage, symptoms related to other medical or psychological problems (14, 15, 16) Need a series of visits – often co-operation with a doctor – sometimes a referral to a hospital

Chapter 4

Questions and Answers

how the book can help dental patients

A nybody who has a serious health problem is likely to want to ask questions about the problem and how it can be treated. In the case of dental problems the main person to answer such questions must be the dentist, but it must also be quite common for people to ask friends, family etc. in order to find out if anyone else has experienced a similar problem and if so what happened to them. Another important use of this book is to help dental patients by supplying an additional source of information that can provide answers to their questions about dental problems and treatments. In this chapter seven common questions are given together with outline answers. Each answer then contains extensive references to other relevant parts of the book.

All of these seven questions are about dental situations where the patient has a choice, though in two cases the choice is whether to have treatment or not. There are of course very many other questions that dental patients might have, but it would be impossible to cover them all in this chapter. The way that the questions in this chapter have been answered by including references to other parts of the book should help readers to find answers to other questions that they might have. This chapter therefore provides readers with another way of starting to use the book.

Question 1: *Do I have a choice of filling material when a tooth needs a filling?*
The answer to this question is basically 'yes', but could be 'no' if you are not prepared to pay for particular expensive options, or if your dentist does not offer some options. The reasons why the answer cannot be straightforward are made clear in Chapter 9 which discusses fillings in detail, but will also be briefly outlined here. The four main types of filling material in general use are as follows: amalgam, white composite, glass ionomer cement, and gold, with a fifth and newer filling material being porcelain (see Chapter 16). If you choose gold or porcelain you will have to pay for these expensive alternatives and you may also have to find a dentist that offers them. Glass ionomer cement is only used in special circumstances, so the main choice that dental patients are likely

to be offered is between amalgam and white composite.

As a general rule for NHS treatment, white composite can only be used where the filling shows, i.e. on front teeth. This rule means that fillings on back teeth, funded in whole or in part by the NHS, have to be made with amalgam. There is, however, some controversy about the use of amalgam fillings because amalgam contains mercury. If anybody would rather not have amalgam fillings then they can choose white composite in nearly all cases, but if they do make such a choice, then the treatment which includes the filling cannot include any NHS element, and so will have to be paid for entirely by the patient.

Question 2: *When can I choose between having a tooth extracted or having it root filled and crowned?*
The basic answer to this question is that you should have a choice of root canal treatment as an alternative to extraction on nearly every occasion when the root of a tooth has become infected. Chapter 10 will help readers who are not clear what root canal treatment is for and how it is applied. A full answer to this question forms part of Chapters 10 and 11, but the causes of the problem and an outline of possibilities of choice are given here.

At the centre of every tooth is a section called the root canal, and some teeth have more than one root canal as described in Chapter 6 (see Figure 6.1 in particular). Infection of the root canal normally follows damage to a tooth when it has become decayed due to the tooth disease caries. If left untreated the infection of the root canal can soon also cause an abscess which appears on the gum, and which is usually very painful. If the tooth is badly damaged it may also need crowning, but even then you can usually have the tooth treated rather than extracted. This, however, is not always possible, because there are complications which can affect the decision on treatment.

There is, however, an underlying principle which all dental patients should understand. This principle is that in theory extraction should always be seen as a last resort, so that every other treatment possibility which might save the tooth should be tried first. Unfortunately applying this principle in every case is not always sensible, partly because of the expense to the patient, but also because the chances of other treatments being successful can be limited. In the case of root canal treatment, there is something like a 15% chance of failure within a year and the treatment is only likely to last for between 5 and 25 years. One advantage that extraction does have is that it supplies a quick fix. If the patient is suffering considerable pain because of an abscess then extraction will supply immediate relief, whereas root canal treatment will take time during which there may still be some pain.

There are four teeth which it is sometimes not sensible to try to save by root canal treatment. These are the so called 'wisdom teeth', those numbered 8 on the chart in Figure 7.1. Extraction is often the only sensible choice for these particular teeth for two reasons. The first is that the root systems for these teeth are often twisted and so difficult to treat, and the second is that, as extraction of these teeth will not cause a gap, then eating efficiency is not impaired in any way. Apart from these four teeth root canal treatment is a possibility for remedial treatment as an alternative to extraction. It must also be remembered that though extraction might give solve the problem quickly in the short term, the long-term effects of extraction can be considerable. Gaps caused by extractions have to be filled, either with a denture or a bridge, both of which have their own disadvantages (see Chapter 11). If a tooth has to be crowned as well as having root canal treatment then this usually requires a post to be cemented in the root canal as an anchor for the crown (see Chapter 10). Case studies 6,8,9 and 10 in Chapter 5 all illustrate treatments involving crowns and dentures.

It is certainly true that dental patients who are already aware of the alternatives are very keen to avoid extractions for as long as possible, and will put pressure on their dentists to use alternatives like root canal treatment. The availability of root canal treatment in general dental practice in the UK is relatively new, having grown over the last twenty or thirty years, but even now many teeth are extracted that could be saved with root canal treatment.

Question 3: *Is it possible for me to choose between either a bridge or a partial denture to fill a space left by an extraction. What are the pros and cons of each?*

The answer to this question is not entirely straightforward but the basic answer to the question as it is worded is almost certainly 'yes'. Chapter 11 discusses the details of extractions and the difference between bridges and dentures, but a brief outline answer to the question is given here. The wording of the question in this case is important because the words 'an extraction' imply that it is only one tooth that has been extracted. Normally a single gap can easily be filled with either a bridge or a partial denture. In many cases it will be suggested that the fitting of a bridge is postponed until the tissues disturbed by the extraction have settled down. The treatment then is usually to fit a temporary partial denture and then switch to a bridge after a wait of about six months.

If a patient has a single gap, or even two or three separate single gaps, then they are likely to find bridges preferable to partial dentures. The main reason for this is that bridges feel more natural as they stay permanently in place and do not have supporting plates which are an ever-present extra object in the mouth. The main drawbacks of bridges are firstly that they are more expensive than partial dentures, and secondly that healthy teeth have to be used as anchors for the bridge. These healthy teeth will need to be shaped in order to provide a secure anchorage for the bridge, and this shaping often entails removing healthy tissue. Such teeth will also have more work to do during the eating process. Bridges that fill gaps of two or more teeth need a much more complex design and are therefore even more expensive.

If either bridges or dentures are fitted than extra care over cleaning will have to be taken. The presence of a bridge often creates extra spaces between the bridge and other teeth or gums and these may need different cleaning techniques. Dentures need to be cleaned regularly. With dentures there can be particular problems that occur on the surface of the mouth under the plate of the denture. The most effective ways of avoiding such problems are to clean this space on a regular after-food basis, to rest the mouth surface by removing the denture at night, and to avoid too much sugar in food and drink. Chapter 11 has full details about fitting bridges and dentures and the choice between them. Case Studies 6,8 and 10 in Chapter 5 illustrate aspects of the use of bridges and dentures.

Question 4: *Is there any way in which Dad can have a better fitting denture?*

If anyone has a relative who has full dentures and these dentures are causing problems such as seeming insecure or not being easy to use for eating and also if the person concerned has not been to see a dentist for several years, then it is almost certain that a better result could be achieved by modifying the present dentures, or fitting new dentures, or just possibly by carrying out minor oral surgery. It is fairly natural for people to think that once all their teeth have been removed then there will be no more changes in their mouth. Unfortunately this is quite wrong, because the nature of the tissue which supports teeth (see Chapter 6) means that it will go on changing for many years after the teeth have been extracted. Such changes will then affect the fit of the dentures and make them much less effective. People with full dentures should certainly visit their dentist on at least an annual basis. Chapter 11 has the details about full dentures. Case Study 12 in Chapter 5 is a typical case of problems caused because the person concerned had full dentures and had not been to a dentist for many years. Case Study 11 in Chapter 5 illustrates an expensive way of achieving a modern alternative to a normal full denture.

Question 5: *What kinds of dental problems are special to teenagers, who needs orthodontic treatment and how does it work?*

Dental problems for teenagers can arise because of their particular physical stage of development. They can also suffer dental problems because they follow a particular lifestyle associated with the nature of the teenage years, excessive dieting for example. The range of teenager problems is discussed under the expectations for the 11 to 15 age range in Chapter 2.

The main reason for the inclusion of this question in this chapter concerns the physical development of teeth. During the early teenage years the remainder of the permanent teeth (apart from the wisdom teeth) grow into position. The way that permanent teeth position themselves in the jaw and in relation to each other depends on 'genes' and also on the previous condition of the first teeth. Big teeth in a small jaw, teeth that grow in the wrong part of the gum, and teeth that protrude forwards instead of fitting snugly onto the teeth in the opposite jaw, are all very common problems. Around half of the teenage population has some problems of this nature, though many of these are not serious enough to need treatment. In this book all such conditions are put under the heading of 'misaligned teeth'. Treatment that is concerned with misaligned teeth is officially known as 'orthodontic treatment'.

There are two main reasons why teenagers with misaligned teeth are offered orthodontic treatment. The first is to improve eating efficiency and the second is to improve appearance. The second of these reasons in particular requires a measure of good judgement, as what may be an improvement in appearance to one person might seem like a loss of individuality to another person. Orthodontic treatment can take up to two years to complete and often needs dedication and a tough-minded attitude to teasing by the teenager concerned. When orthodontic treatment is being considered the knowledge of the details given in this book could be particularly helpful to teenagers and their parents. Chapter 13 contains these details. Case Studies 2, 4 and 5 in Chapter 5 illustrate very clearly the nature of the physical problems, the judgements concerning the necessity for treatment, and possible personal problems associated with the nature of orthodontic treatment.

Question 6: *Is it sometimes sensible to pay for private treatment rather than to use the NHS scheme? If so, how much does it cost and is there an insurance scheme that would be best for me and my family?*
This question involves some fairly complex issues and these are discussed in detail in Chapter 18. A relatively simple answer to the first part of this question is that it may be sensible to pay for private treatment under certain conditions, but paying for a whole family with some children under 18 is less likely to be a sensible option at present, as the treatment for under 18s which was completely free under the NHS would then have to be paid for under private registration. For individuals who already pay 80% of all the NHS treatment they receive it is sensible to stay with the same dentist even if this dentist stops treating patients on the NHS.

For many people in the UK the question of leaving the NHS scheme will have added urgency over the next few years because many dentists are ceasing to offer treatment under the NHS scheme. Such dentists may well offer patients on their list the choice of going private or finding another dentist who does treat patients under the NHS scheme. Other people who might have to make a decision on the choice of NHS or private treatment are those looking for a change of dentist for particular reasons such as moving house, or increased income, or children leaving home. Suggestions for factors to consider when choosing a dentist are also given in Chapter 18.

There are three basic methods of paying for private treatment which are: (1) paying from your own funds as needed, (2) belonging to an insurance scheme, (3) working for a company which has an employee dental treatment scheme. Insurance schemes come in two different forms, the most common being 'capitation' schemes. For capitation schemes it is the dentist who registers with the scheme so that if you wish to be registered with a certain dental practice then you will have no other choice of capitation scheme. You can however choose to use the other type of insurance scheme where you pay the bills and then claim all or a proportion back from the insurer. The details of companies that offer these two forms of insurance are given in Chapter 18.

There are likely to be particular advantages in being with a private practice. The dentists in such practices generally take more time over discussion and treatment, they might also offer a greater range of treatments and have more incentive to try the relatively innovative treatments which can improve both results and the patient experience. Some of these innovative treatments are described in Chapters 15 and 16. Private practices are also likely to be more customer oriented, with comfortable premises and add on services like free coffee or tea for patients who are waiting for appointments.

Question 7: *Is there a new treatment not generally available that could help me?*

The answer to this question could well be 'yes' if you have certain particular dental problems, for example if you suffer from dentophobia, i.e. if you find it extremely difficult to receive any kind of dental treatment. For such people there is the possibility of receiving treatment that does not involve injections and is much less intrusive in terms of objects and fingers being inserted in the mouth. Some dentophobics can also be helped by hypnosis. Many of these possibilities are discussed in Chapter 16. Another example of where one of the newer treatment can help is the use of implants which basically replace extracted teeth with artificial teeth that are fixed into the bone of the jaw. Implants are described in detail in Chapter 15 and Case Study 11 in Chapter 5 describes how implants helped a particular individual.

Generally speaking there are very few of these newer treatments that are available from NHS sources. If people qualify for free treatment under the NHS, and are then referred to a dental hospital for a particular problem, then they may well be offered an innovative treatment. Everybody else is likely to have to pay for these newer treatments, which often are expensive.

Chapter 5

Case Studies

twelve personal experiences of dental treatment

The main purpose of this chapter is to use case studies to give readers a possible comparison with their own situations, or with the situations of family or friends. The case studies also give examples of the ways that dental problems and treatments can interact with peoples' personalities and lifestyles. References to later chapters are given at the end of each case study so that readers can follow it up by checking on the detail of the problems and treatments involved.

This chapter also illustrates the point that an important element of dental treatment is that it is people that are being treated, and not just teeth and mouths. The personal element can sometimes be neglected in dental treatment. Four aspects of the personal element are considered in these case studies as follows: (1) It sometimes happens that problems with the appearance of teeth and mouths arise because an emergency treatment in the past has dealt with an immediate problem with a tooth, and the long term effects on the person have not been taken into account. (2) Often it can be a person's lifestyle that has contributed towards a problem. (3) Dental treatment can make a major difference in enhancing or reducing a person's self image and confidence. (4) Fear of going to a dentist can also be very strong. Some people probably feel very brave just reading this book!

All of these studies are based on real people, though some cases are derived from a mixture of more than one real case. The case studies are given in an age related order as that might help readers to find one that is relevant to an immediate interest. The names used are not the real names of the people concerned. A description of the person and their personality is given as this background very often puts the problem and treatment into a context that is vital in order to see the point of the study. The physical descriptions are different from the real characters.

Case Study 1: Anthony – age 5
This case illustrates how other medical and human factors can interact with dental problems and treatments.

Anthony has dark curly hair, big dark eyes, and is small for his age. He has always been rather sickly, suffering from chest problems that have been given long term treatment with steroids and antibiotics. His parents are separated and Anthony lives with his mother who has always been particularly concerned to support and comfort him. His dental problems are directly related to this history. Early medicines were administered in a syrup in order to make them palatable for a baby, and other comforts included sweet drinks and chocolates etc.

An appointment was made for Anthony because he was suffering from severe toothache. He had been finding it difficult to sleep because of this toothache. When he came for the appointment he needed much persuasion before his teeth could be examined, with tears and sobbing and appeals to his mother. After agreeing to sit in the chair he was then very co-operative; being examined by a man in a white coat was obviously a fairly common experience for him.

Unfortunately it transpired that Anthony was a classic case of severe caries of the deciduous (or first) teeth caused by prolonged contact with sweet liquids at an early age. The diagram showing the positions of deciduous teeth is Figure 2.1, and it can be seen that the total number of deciduous teeth is twenty, ten upper and ten lower. Anthony had such severe caries in 14 of these teeth that they could not be saved. Extraction was the only possibility.

In a case such as this, where more than two teeth are to be extracted, the operation has to be done under a general anaesthetic. At the time of this diagnosis Anthony was still under strong medication and could not receive a general anaesthetic, which meant a few more weeks of the pain which could only be alleviated through painkillers. The operation was eventually carried out successfully, but was very traumatic for Anthony and his mother. Any operation under a general anaesthetic causes the patient to suffer from some element of shock. In this case the mouth would also be very sore for two or more weeks. Artificial replacements for deciduous teeth are not generally possible, so Anthony's appearance and eating efficiency were both affected; this situation will only change when his second teeth appear. Deciduous teeth also play a part in positioning second teeth so that Anthony's dental condition will have to be monitored very carefully over the next few years. The prognosis can still be positive, as long as he generates good habits for eating, drinking and tooth care.

Details about the causes and prevention of caries are given in Chapter 6; extractions are dealt with in Chapter 11.

Case Study 2: James – age 11
This case illustrates how treatments sometimes have to be modified because of other factors. In this case the factor concerned appears to be a physical reaction, but this reaction could well be associated with the young person's

psychological background.

James is normal height for his age but is overweight. He likes computer games rather than football. He is reasonably good at talking to adults and certainly wants to be a part of the decision-making process for possible treatments. The main difficulty in providing dental treatment for James is that he cannot stand having anything in his mouth apart from food and drink. Even the process of inserting fingers and the instruments involved in dental examination causes him considerable distress.

James came to the surgery with an orthodontic problem. His teeth were overcrowded because the teeth were too large for the jaw. This is a common problem which can affect people in various different ways. In order to appreciate the way James was affected you need to refer to Figure 7.2 and also look at your own teeth in a mirror. For James his overcrowding was forcing the canines forwards out of the mouth. The canines form the boundary between incisors and molars and therefore are very much a part of a normal appearance. The normal treatment for this condition is to extract the first premolars and to fit an appliance to bring the canines back into the mouth. For James with his reaction problem, an orthodontic appliance was out of the question. As an alternative treatment the four canines were extracted. After about three months the spaces had been filled and the other teeth had lined up in a reasonably normal fashion. Both James and his parents were pleased at this result.

Details about the causes and treatment for orthodontic problems are given in Chapter 13; extractions are dealt with in Chapter 11.

Case Study 3: Tracy – age 11

This case illustrates two main points. The first point is that many young people whose teeth are still in a process of change receive accidental damage. As tooth and mouth development is still happening the situation often needs extra special care. A common way of achieving this special care is for the young person to visit a specialist orthodontist who gives advice on the treatment. After this specialist consultation, the actual treatment is then carried out by the person's own dentist.

Tracy is lively, attractive and healthy and has a friendly outgoing personality. Her parents are caring and both of them have professional occupations. Tracy was in her last year at primary school. One day as she was playing in the school yard during morning break she slipped and fell awkwardly so that her mouth received a nasty blow. This blow caused very severe damage to an upper central incisor with most of it being broken into pieces and disturbed from the socket. Her mouth was also badly cut. Tracy was taken to a hospital immediately after the accident. She needed two stitches in her mouth and was advised to see her dentist either that day or the next.

Tracy had always been to her dentist for regular checks on the progress of her teeth. Her dentist had been able to build up a good relationship with her and she was very good at listening to his explanations and responding to treatment. When she went for her appointment after the accident an X-ray soon revealed that there were no remnants of the tooth in the root space. The loss of an upper central incisor gives a gap that is very noticeable and treatment needs to deal with this gap as soon as possible. For the moment Tracy was advised to let the gum and lip heal before further treatment, and she was given another appointment for the next week to allow time for the injuries to heal.

At the next appointment the dentist had a discussion with Tracy about the nature of her treatment now and in the future. The gap needed to be filled immediately both because of the effect on appearance and to hold the teeth into place. Because of her age there might be orthodontic problems arising from teeth moving sideways in the jaw as they developed, so she would need to visit an orthodontic specialist. Any appliances to fill the gap and perform orthodontic functions would be in the form of dentures until she was around seventeen. At that age all of her teeth except the wisdom teeth would have appeared. The jaw and the positions of the teeth in the jaw would then be stable so it would be possible for her to have a bridge which would be more like having the natural tooth directly replaced.

Although still upset about her loss, Tracy co-operated very well in the procedures for making and fitting the partial denture and was very pleased with the appearance of the resulting artificial tooth. After another two months she visited a dental hospital to see the orthodontic specialist. After the consultation with the specialist, Tracy was fitted with a more complex appliance that would hold her first molars in place, so avoiding overcrowding problems as well as filling the gap.

Details about the causes, treatment and prevention of accidental damage are given in Chapter 14 and the procedures for dental first aid are given in Chapter 17. The fitting of dentures and bridges is dealt with in Chapter 11.

Case Study 4: Janine – age 14

Both this case and the next are concerned with orthodontic problems and the age group of 13-15 which is mainly affected. Because we are dealing with teenagers, a period in life when young people often have many other worries, and because treatment is mainly concerned with affects on appearance, discussions and decisions on this treatment can be difficult. As treatment needs dedication and perseverance, success often depends on the personality of the patient.

Janine has fair hair and green eyes, and is average height and weight for her age. She has a pleasant calm personality, listens carefully and responds well by asking sensible questions. She is very well supported by a caring family. Her appearance was badly affected by the way her teeth had developed in the last year and she made an appointment to come with her mother to discuss possible treatments. Janine's problem was severe 'buck teeth'. Referring to Figure 13.1, her upper central incisors had an overjet and an overbite that were well over double average measurements. Because of the excess protrusion, there can be a considerable chance of damage to the incisors in cases like this and Janine was also very distressed about her appearance; young people of this age can be cruel in their remarks and she was suffering a lot of teasing.

Treatment in such a case is fairly standard and involves extractions plus a two-year period of wearing orthodontic appliances. The incisors need room in order to retract, so the upper first premolars have to be extracted. An upper orthodontic appliance is needed to retract the upper incisors and a lower orthodontic appliance is needed to suppress the lower incisors. The details of how these appliances are fitted and adjusted are given in Chapter 13. Treatment by the dentist is long and quite wearing for the patient and day-to-day care of the appliance is vital and needs perseverance and dedication. In Janine's case she had motivation, a sensible pragmatic approach to dealing with the situation and the vital backup from her family.

Even for someone like Janine the process has a human cost as illustrated by an incident about two months after the appliances had been fitted. About a week before a normal check up visit Janine's mother phoned the surgery and was obviously in some distress. She said that Janine had been in tears over the last two or three days. She asked if she could she come with Janine on the next visit and could some way be found of giving them both some extra encouragement to cope with the stress of dealing with the human consequences of the treatment. Luckily the dental practice concerned kept some 'before' and 'after' photographs and one of the cases illustrated started with a situation very similar to Janine's. In that case the 'after' photo showed a girl who was looking very pretty and very obviously pleased with the change in her appearance. Janine cried again when she saw those pictures, but the tears seemed more for relief than for her current problems. Her mother also had a private word with the dentist and indicated that Janine was encountering a difficult patch in other ways as well; having to cope with the appearance of the appliances and their day-to-day care had been the last straw.

After that incident there were no more major problems and the result after two years was a much improved appearance. Janine was delighted and reported that her school mates were now making complimentary remarks rather than teasing her as before. She also fully understood that the positions of the teeth in question would need very careful monitoring over the next four or five years.

Details about the causes and treatment of orthodontic problems are given in Chapter 13.

Case Study 5: Victoria (always called 'Viccy') – age 14

This case, like the last case of Janine, concerns orthodontic treatment. In this case the problem was not so severe and the personality and lifestyle of the young person were very different. There can be cases where some imperfection in the shape and positioning of teeth can seem natural and sometimes can be said to enhance the appearance by giving an element of difference and individuality. A noticeable gap between to two top central incisors is fairly common. As long as there is no impairment of eating efficiency, or an enhanced possibility of damage, then leaving well alone in such case is sometimes a reasonable option. This case illustrates a borderline for whether to treat or not, which was resolved first one way and then another.

Viccy is relatively tall and above average weight, though certainly not fat. She has a friendly personality, with a great sense of humour and a passion for horse riding which everybody seems to know about very quickly. She is also very bright and is obviously destined for university and a professional career. Viccy has very healthy teeth, but as her main teeth had erupted and positioned themselves, some crowding had occurred in the upper front teeth. The cause of the crowding was the resistance of one of the upper canines to moving back on the jaw where there was some space before the first premolar (see Figure 7.2). Normally the pressure of the lips is enough to push the canines into place but in Viccy's case this was not happening. During a normal check-up visit the dentist discussed the situation with Viccy and indicated that a possible treatment would be to fit a simple upper removable orthodontic appliance. No extractions would be necessary and the treatment would probably last about a year. After discussions with her parents Viccy decided to go ahead with this treatment. The appliance was fitted successfully and Viccy learnt how to fit and remove the appliance and also how to look after it. She was also told that regular monthly appointments were a necessary part of the treatment.

The next time the dentist saw Viccy it was for an entirely different problem and was some five months after the fitting of the appliance. It was immediately obvious that Viccy's teeth were in the same state as before and closer examination showed that the back teeth had grown forward to fill the space that had previously been available for the canine to move into. Nothing could now be done to deal with the overcrowding without extracting at least two teeth. Using the present appliance would now have no effect at all.

Viccy seemed a bit concerned about the trouble taken and the waste of time. When pressed she laughed and said that she did persevere for a week or two but found the care and use of the appliance too much of a chore and difficult to fit into her busy lifestyle, in particular with the early morning care of her horse. Apparently the final straw had been a comment from her best friend that Viccy wouldn't be Viccy with near perfect teeth so why did she bother.

Details about the causes and treatment of orthodontic problems are given in Chapter 13.

Case Study 6: Sally – age 23

There are times when dental treatment is carried out for reasons other than problems due to disease, damage, or misplacement. An extreme example would be someone who wanted two diamonds permanently fixed to their upper front incisors because they thought it would enhance their image. Sally's case is not quite so extreme, but it does provide an example of a situation where the request for treatment for non-medical reasons is perfectly valid, even if it is also rather amusing.

Sally is an attractive and articulate person, who had been with the same dentist for most of her life. She therefore knew her dentist well and felt able to explain her problem to him even if it was rather unusual. Sally has healthy and well shaped teeth, but suffered an accident as a child which resulted in the loss of two adjacent teeth. These teeth had been replaced with artificial teeth fastened to a denture. The artificial teeth were a perfect match to her other teeth, Sally has a very attractive smile and certainly no one would know she had a denture unless she told them about it. Sally's problem was that she had just acquired a new boyfriend. She was obviously very much in love with this boyfriend and confided that she hoped they might eventually form a permanent partnership. Her present problem was that both she and the new boyfriend enjoyed passionate kissing and she was worried that in the course of this part of their lovemaking her denture might become displaced. Apparently there had been some risk of this event happening already, which had caused her to call a temporary halt to proceedings at a time when she might have been expected to have become even more involved.

The solution to this problem was relatively easy, even if it was also expensive. The denture was replaced by a five unit bridge, that is a bridge with three abutments and two pontics. As Sally had very healthy teeth, such a bridge would with sensible care be likely to last for twenty years or more. As a permanent structure, which could not be displaced, it was also the answer to Sally's present problem and Sally was delighted with the result. Two years later during a routine visit she announced that she was pregnant and confirmed that the father was the boyfriend concerned previously.

Details about the fitting of dentures and bridges are given in Chapter 11.

Case Study 7: Pete – age 23

This case is an illustration of the fact that everybody is subject to gum disease all the time. It is only good personal hygiene (cleaning teeth etc.) and regular visits to the dentist that keeps the disease at bay.

Pete is a strong and healthy young man with a friendly cheerful personality. His job is a mix of delivery and sales and he evidently enjoys the fun and companionship that men of his age often have. Regular dental hygiene and regular visits to the dentist have not been a part of his lifestyle. He confessed that he had not been to a dentist for at least ten years and that he was only here now at the insistence of a new girlfriend.

The first symptom that was evident was bad breath, so no wonder the girlfriend had insisted on this visit. Pete also had swollen gums that bled very easily under pressure, but his teeth were all still firmly in place. His symptoms were therefore those of chronic gingivitis. This disease, at this stage, is relatively rare for this age group but can occur and worsen quickly given a consistent lack of care.

Pete's treatment consisted of the scaling of all of his teeth and as they were so badly affected this process took two visits of half an hour each and needed an injection each time. He was also put on a course of antibiotics and told to have regular hot salt water mouthwashes three or more times each day. He was also very firmly told the cause of his problems and that they were typical for tramps living rough but not for someone who is adequately housed. Buying a good toothbrush and using it regularly would help his image in terms of being nice to be close to. Luckily Pete kept his sense of humour through all this and later reported with a big grin that his treatment had been a great success in progressing his relationship with the new girlfriend.

Details about the causes, treatment and prevention of advanced gum disease are given in Chapters 6 and 12.

Case Study 8: Shirley – age 45

Neglect of dental care and the effect on health and appearance can take many forms. Very often the neglect does not seem to have any serious effect at all in the short term, but the long term effects can build up until something triggers a realisation that there is a relatively serious problem. This case is an example of such a situation, where personal dental hygiene was good but dental treatment was only sought intermittently and then only to deal with emergencies. The subsequent treatments were also only given to deal with the immediate problems as presented.

Shirley is a slim woman of average height. She has dark hair with some strands of grey appearing. She has six children and her husband left her soon after the birth of the last child some five years ago. Shirley had been accompanying some of her children on dental visits during the eighteen months that they had been registered with this practice, but had never made an appointment for herself. She had specifically said to the dental assistant on one occasion that she had no problems with her teeth so did not need an appointment. One day, however, she did make an appointment, but did not indicate on the phone to the receptionist that the appointment was for anything in particular. When Shirley appeared for the appointment she seemed rather embarrassed and said that she would not have bothered the dentist but that her sister was on a visit. This sister had not seen Shirley for about four years and had told Shirley that she was shocked by her changed appearance and that Shirley ought to visit her dentist.

Even just by looking at Shirley's face it was evident that her sister had some reason for her comments. The general appearance of the teeth was uneven and her cheeks were not symmetrical. Examination of the teeth showed that the upper right incisors (1&2 in Figure 7.2) had crowns that were a slightly different shade from the natural teeth and each other; they were also slightly longer than the corresponding natural left side incisors. Shirley also had three missing teeth. These were adjacent upper teeth numbered left 4,5,6 in Figure 7.2. Such a gap causes the inside of the cheek to develop into the space over time so that the outside of the cheek then shows a considerable indentation. Shirley said that the two crowns had been fitted some twelve years ago, in the middle of one of her pregnancies, and that the teeth had been extracted separately as emergencies by different dentists. Two of these dentists had said that she ought to have a denture but she had responded by saying that she did not have time to spare for making the necessary appointments.

Whatever her sister had said to her must have had a considerable effect because Shirley agreed to have the necessary remedial treatment. This treatment consisted of replacing the crowns with some that were an exact match in size and colour with the natural left-hand incisors. As Shirley's teeth were healthy enough to support a bridge, the three-tooth gap was filled with such a bridge. The result was quite remarkable, almost a transformation. The restored balance to the shape of the cheeks made Shirley's face at rest look much softer. The fact that when she smiled and laughed her teeth looked fine seemed to have made her smile and laugh much more readily. She really did seem like a changed person and on her last check-up visit became quite emotional when she thanked the dentist.

Details about fitting crowns are given in Chapter 10, and the fitting of bridges is dealt with in Chapter 11.

Case Study 9: Dennis – age 47

In some ways the dental treatment in this case is a relatively minor issue. What this case illustrates is the fact that if a patient has some knowledge about what dental treatments might be possible then, following constructive discussions with their dentist, they can sometimes obtain treatments that are special for their case. The idea of making patients more knowledgeable and therefore more articulate about their dental needs is a major purpose of this book. The case also illustrates the fact that the vast majority of dentists would like their patients to be more knowledgeable. The terrified, not-wanting-to-know patient often passes their stress on to the dentist. By contrast a good working discussion with a patient, who then knows what to expect, is likely to result in treatment which is much more relaxed and so much easier for both the dentist and the patient.

Dennis is tall and thin, well educated and with a responsible job in local government. He is obviously used to being involved in decision-making and has firm ideas about how his dental treatment should progress in his middle age. One of his back teeth, lower left 6 in Figure 7.2, was giving him considerable trouble. This tooth had been heavily filled over the years and now had an infected pulp, so giving pain and an abscess. After examination and taking an X-ray the dentist and Dennis discussed possible treatments. Dennis was keen to keep the tooth, especially as he had not yet had any extractions, and asked about root filling and a crown. The dentist showed Dennis the X-ray which indicated that two of the three roots of the tooth were very distorted and could not therefore be root filled. The simplest solution would certainly be to extract the tooth. Dennis saw what the problem was but was still unwilling to have the tooth extracted. With someone like Dennis the dentist did not have to appear infallible and always able to give an instant set of all possible ways forward, so it was suggested that Dennis had a course of antibiotics and that the dentist would think about the case and consult other dentist colleagues to see if there were any sensible alternatives to extraction.

As a result of this longer consideration a relatively simple solution was discussed and agreed. The tooth would be cut into two parts, one part attached to the two distorted roots and the other part attached to the treatable root. The first part would then be extracted and the other part root filled and crowned. The result was a smaller tooth, but almost as efficient for eating. The gaps between this tooth and adjacent teeth were larger but not enough to be noticeable without a close inspection. With the root in place the ridge keeps its shape and Dennis was therefore right to be concerned not to lose the tooth if it was at all possible. With luck, it would still be another ten or more years before he lost any teeth.

Details about root canal treatment and crowns are given in Chapter 10, and the effects of extractions are dealt with in Chapter 11.

Case Study 10: Olga – age 55

This case has some similarities with Shirley (Case Study 8); they are both middle- aged women who have neglected their teeth. The main difference is that Olga's situation is very much worse than Shirley's. There were special circumstances in this case, but one conclusion that can be drawn is that people in the UK are very fortunate to have the availability of good dental support services. The case clearly demonstrates what the consequences could be if these services were not there or if an individual never used them.

Olga was brought to the surgery by her daughter. This daughter was a regular visitor to the practice and is an attractive and vivacious young woman. By contrast Olga's appearance was really quite shocking. The main factor that caused her strange appearance was that the space between her chin and nose had evidently contracted. Her mouth had also shrunk and she had hollow cheeks so giving an almost 'witch-like' image. Her daughter said that Olga had lived very poorly in a remote part of the ex-Eastern bloc countries for the last twenty years, and only now had been able to leave in order to have a prolonged stay with her daughter in England.

Examination of Olga's mouth showed that she had lost many back teeth and the upper incisors were badly worn. It was largely this second feature that was causing the contraction of the mouth space so bringing the chin closer to the nose. None of the extracted teeth had been replaced by artificial teeth and the treatment for Olga's condition was reasonably straightforward. Any remaining teeth that were healthy were crowned. These included the upper incisors. As there were enough healthy teeth to provide support, it was also possible to fit partial dentures to replace the other missing teeth. Olga would end up with a full set of natural and artificial teeth, and her appearance would therefore return to normal.

The total time taken for this treatment was nearly three months. As Olga did not have any English, all questions and instructions had to be relayed through the daughter. From being fairly obviously terrified Olga gradually relaxed, especially as she began to realise the possible benefits of the treatment. When Olga did start to relax, some of the problems of translation made mother and daughter laugh together and the explanation of the problem to the dentist made him laugh as well. In this case the result of the treatment was definitely a transformation; from looking more like a woman in her late 70s or 80s, Olga now almost looked younger than her age, especially when she laughed or smiled. Olga had also found the confidence to start to use cosmetics and this made a considerable difference as well. The dentist tried a joke: 'You now look more like sisters than mother and daughter'. When translated this seemed to cause great hilarity in them both, with a great torrent of comment from Olga. The daughter explained that Olga was jokingly saying that with her new appearance she could now look for a new husband, although her remarks had been a bit more down-to-earth than that. If this case has a moral, it is perhaps that we are lucky now to be able to live longer and to stay looking much younger than our forbears of even 100 years ago, but even then we should not take all advances for granted; we have to take responsibilities for our own care as well.

Details about fitting crowns are given in Chapter 10, and the fitting of partial dentures is dealt with in Chapter 11.

Case Study 11: George age 59

This case has a major difference to the others in that while the problem is fairly common, the solution suggested involves relatively new and expensive techniques.

George is a successful business man. He keeps himself fit and always has a slight tan, which looks as though it is kept in place at considerable expense. He obviously takes a pride in his appearance which he regards as important for making a suitable impression on his business contacts. Unfortunately George has suffered a series of dental problems which have left him edentulous (i.e. without any natural teeth). His natural teeth have been replaced with a very good set of dentures. These dentures are good in the sense that they have been matched to the colour and shape of his ex-natural teeth and, as a consequence, no one would know he was wearing dentures from his appearance, even when he smiles or laughs. George has another problem, however, which is the state of his upper dental bearing ridge. This is the ridge that used to contain the teeth. In George's case this ridge was poorly defined, which meant that there was a possibility of failure in the air seal necessary for supporting the upper denture (see Chapter 11). Such a failure causes the upper denture to drop into the mouth cavity. This is a relatively common problem; it can be overcome to some extent by using special adhesives but these can be difficult and time-consuming to apply and even then are not always successful. As can be imagined, for someone like George this problem had the possibility of creating hugely embarrassing situations.

In order to solve this problem his present upper denture would be replaced by an overdenture. The overdenture would be fastened to four implants strategically placed in the upper ridge. The overdenture would just clip on to the four implants and would be firmly held in place. This treatment can cost over £5000 and lasts for about a year, but George had no hesitation in opting for it. When it was complete George was immensely pleased with the result.

The basis of the treatment suggested for George is given in Chapter 15.

Case Study 12: Fred – age 76

This case is an illustration of a psychological problem rather than a dental problem. In more down-to-earth terms it is dealing with a state of mind, trying to change the attitude of someone who has fixed ideas. It is fairly natural for older people to resist change by saying that in the short time they have left making changes is not worthwhile. Very often, however, such changes can greatly enhance the quality of the older person's life and, almost as importantly, improve their interactions with others. Being sufficiently persuasive and finding a suitable 'trigger' to institute change is often the major difficulty in these cases.

Fred is short and skinny, he has bright blue eyes and a friendly, cheerful personality. He spent 27 years in the army and then worked as an odd job man in a department store until retiring late at the age of 67. His wife had died about five years previously and for most of the time since then he had lived on his own in the family home. About four months ago he had sold his house and moved into a residential home. Fred was accompanied on his first visit to the dentist by Frank who was another old soldier living in the same residential home. Frank also insisted on coming in to the consultation with the dentist. Fred's dental problem was immediately obvious: He had full dentures that were almost totally ineffective; he had difficulty in keeping them in place even when talking; the problems he must have had in eating did not bear thinking about. The consultation with Frank intervening was really quite funny. Frank kept on saying that Fred was a 'silly old fool. He's had those dentures twenty or more years'. The friendship between the two was, however, evident. Fred was laughing too and did not need much persuasion to be treated with a new set of dentures.

The dentist explained how the ridges contracted over the years and that the new dentures would precisely fit the present state of Fred's ridges and mouth cavities; the new dentures would therefore be enormously more comfortable to wear. Denture technology had also moved on since 1970 and the new dentures could also be made to look very natural, unlike Fred's present dentures. The procedures for measuring, making and fitting full dentures are described in Chapter 11.

When the job was complete, Fred was delighted with his new dentures and said that he realised now that he should have acted years ago. He also said that Frank had told him that other people in the home had been complaining about having to sit near Fred when he was eating, and that was one reason why Frank had put so much pressure on him to get something done. It may well have been the case that others had suggested to Fred in the past that he should seek treatment; the 'trigger' in this case seems to have been the new friendship with a man of roughly the same age and with some of the same background experiences.

Details about the fitting and care of full dentures are given in Chapter 11.

Chapter 6

Basic information

about your teeth, gums and common problems

Summary level

This chapter provides basic knowledge about your teeth and gums. Such knowledge is almost essential if you wish to become fully involved in decision-making about your dental treatment. The chapter gives details of the structure of teeth and gums and the common problems that most people will encounter at some time in their lives. There are also details on how this information can be used for avoiding personal dental problems or dealing with them if they do occur.

This chapter starts by describing how your teeth are made up of different biological substances including enamel, which is not replaced naturally if it is damaged, dentine which causes pain when damaged and pulp which can become infected thus causing even more pain and sometimes an abscess. Supporting structures for teeth include gums and other tissues which provide the socket. The jaw has supporting bone of a specialised nature. Plaque builds up naturally on teeth all the time and has a role in generating tooth decay (caries) and gum disease (gingivitis and periodontitis).

The chapter goes on to describe the progression and treatment of caries: early symptoms are pain with hot and cold substance. A visual inspection at this stage will sometimes show pitting and discolouration of the enamel, left untreated a later symptom is an abscess; treatments for caries range from fillings, to root canal treatment plus crowns, to extraction and replacement with a denture or a bridge.

The chapter also contains a description of the progression and treatment of gum disease: at an early stage gums become red and swollen and bleed under pressure from a tooth brush, at a later stage bone is lost, bad breath is generated and teeth become loose; early treatment is scaling and polishing; later treatment is minor oral surgery or tooth loss. The chapter discusses why everybody suffers to some extent from caries and gum disease, why taking systematic and continuous personal care minimises the effects and why regular visits to the dentist are necessary.

Detailed level

Figure 6.1 is a diagrammatic representation of the basic structure for all teeth. Some teeth have different shapes and some have more than one root, but every tooth has a crown and at least one root and every tooth is constructed with separate sections which consist of different biological substances. These substances are given the names cementum, pulp, dentine and enamel.

The crown of a tooth is the part that shows above the gum. The material of the outer covering of the crown is enamel, which is the hardest substance in the body. Most tissues in the body are self repairing but enamel is not. This means that any damage caused to enamel is permanent. Such damage is most commonly caused by tooth decay, given the official name caries. Damage to enamel can also be caused through physical injury. Enamel is approximately 2 mm thick. Joined on to enamel and as a continuous structure for the surface of

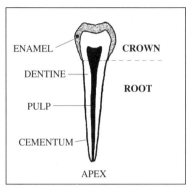

Figure 6.1

the root, except for the point at the very base of the tooth, is a layer of tissue, similar to bone tissue, which is given the name cementum. Immediately underneath the layer of enamel and cementum which together form the outer covering of a tooth, is the part of the tooth containing tissue called dentine. Dentine is sensitive to pain and dental problems often need to be dealt with promptly in order to relieve this pain. In normal use, without any damage, the dentine in the crown is covered by the enamel which acts as a protective shield. Cementum is approximately 1 mm thick and dentine is approximately between 2 and 4 mm thick.

In Figure 6.1, the section shown in black at the centre of the tooth contains the tissue which is given the name pulp. Unlike the substances in the other sections, pulp is a soft tissue which consists of blood vessels and nerves. The outermost part of the pulp is connected to the dentine and has extensions into the dentine like very fine rods known as the dentinal fibrils and it is when these are damaged by decay or treatment by the dentist that the nerves in the pulp are activated to send pain messages to the brain. Another function of the pulp is to repair dentine if it becomes damaged. The pulp also gradually adds dentine over the tooth's life-span so that the section containing the pulp becomes smaller with age. The upper, roughly heart shaped, part of the section shown in black in Figure 6.1 is contained within the crown of the tooth and is called the pulp chamber; the lower part is called the root canal. The root canal is approximately 2 mm thick at its widest section. The point at the base of the tooth is known as the apex. The nerves and blood supply for the pulp chamber run through the apex in a channel known as the apical foramen. This channel is about the width of a fine sewing needle.

At a personal level, knowledge of the structure of teeth should lead to an understanding of why biting on a hard substance causes immediate but relatively slight pain. Pain that is prolonged over a period of time almost certainly means that the enamel has been breached and help is needed.

The teeth are connected to a section of the jaw called the alveolar process. The way that teeth are connected to the alveolar process is shown in Figure 6.2. The cementum (also shown in Figure 6.1) that forms the outer section of the root is in contact with a soft tissue known as the periodontal ligament. The periodontal ligament connects the cementum to the compact bone which forms the outer covering of the alveolar process. The periodontal ligament also acts as a shock absorber for the very considerable forces that apply when the teeth are used for biting and chewing.

The anatomical name for gums is gingiva. The gingiva are attached to the bone of the jaw and fit like a tight collar around each tooth. There is a shallow crevice between the tooth and the gingiva which is known as the gingival crevice. Gums should be firm and pink and the gingival crevice should be barely perceptible.

Now that the basic structure of the teeth, the way that they are connected to the jaw and some of the 'official' terminology has been established, it is possible to describe in detail the nature and cause of the most common dental problems. One common problem is tooth decay, a disease known officially as caries. Another common problem is gum disease

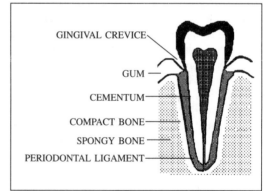

Figure 6.2

which is known officially as gingivitis or at its more advanced stage periodontitis. Both caries and gingivitis are caused by elements in the food we eat. When food and saliva accumulate on the surface of a tooth they form a semi-transparent, yellow/white, tenacious material known as plaque. Plaque tends to gather where there are resting places and it is not removed by natural actions. Examples of such places are crevices in teeth, spaces between teeth and in the gingival crevice. If the top and bottom teeth fit well together, the action of chewing also dislodges plaque, so ill-fitting partial dentures or a damaged filling can also be a cause of plaque accumulation.

The cause of caries is attack on enamel and dentine by an acid formed when bacteria in the mouth react with refined sugar present in plaque. The acid dissolves the enamel and dentine and produces a cavity. Once the acid attack reaches the dentine it generally begins to cause pain. The role of refined sugar in this process needs to be explored further. Caries affects virtually the whole population in communities that eat processed food. By contrast, caries is virtually unknown in primitive communities. The sugar that comes in packets and is present in many processed foods is a carbohydrate that has been refined into a form that does not exist in any quantity in natural foods. This particular form of sugar reacts with the relevant bacteria to produce the acid. Naturally occurring sugars have far less effect.

Under normal circumstances the body has a natural defence for this attack as a component of saliva neutralises the acid after about twenty minutes. During this twenty minutes a microscopic layer of enamel will have been attacked. This process of infiltration by the acid into the enamel is called demineralisation. All is not necessarily lost, however. This is because, after the twenty minutes, when there is no longer any sugar in the plaque, another component of saliva can enter demineralised enamel and generate some partial healing. This process is called remineralisation. As stated earlier, enamel is one of the few body tissues that is not self-replacing. If remineralisation is not allowed to happen then that particular layer of enamel will be lost for ever.

It can be seen from this account of the causes and defences against caries that it is the number and nature of the intakes of sugar that will be a major factor in the onset and severity of caries. With only three intakes of sugar a day as in main meals, remineralisation is likely to be effective in stopping the onset of caries. If there are very many intakes of sugar in a day like, for example, eating sweets frequently, then remineralisation will not have time to work. Many layers of enamel will be lost in each day. The onset of caries will be swift and the disease is likely to progress very quickly. The nature of the food containing sugar is also another factor. Sticky substances like chocolates, sweets and biscuits are much more likely to form plaque than sugar dissolved in hot drinks.

The erosion of many layers of enamel by the acid will eventually penetrate the enamel of the tooth and the acid will then start to attack the dentine. The first indication of a problem with the tooth might then be discomfort with hot or cold food. At this stage a personal inspection will often show that the enamel is pitted and possibly discoloured. As the attack progresses the pain is likely to become continuous and very much more severe. If the caries extends to the pulp it makes the pulp inflamed. This condition is known as pulpitis. Pulpitis is very painful and is likely to lead to the death of the pulp and to be followed by an even worse consequence.

In order to understand what happens next it will be useful to look at Figure 6.2 and imagine what happens when inflammation occurs in the enclosed space, consisting of the pulp chamber and the root canal, that contains the pulp. Inflammation in this enclosed space will cause debris in the form of pus. As this pus is in the enclosed space formed by the pulp chamber and the root canal it causes a considerable build up of pressure and there is nowhere for the pus to go apart from through the channel at the point at the base of the tooth. Remember that this channel is known as the apical foramen and is only as thick as a fine sewing needle. The inflammation then spreads through this channel and begins to affect the periodontal ligament. Once here it causes a condition known as an alveolar or periapical abscess. This abscess causes a throbbing pain and often makes the whole side of the face red and swollen. The temperature of the person can also rise as with a fever. As the periodontal ligament is progressively damaged the tooth will also become loose.

At a personal level the importance of taking action promptly to respond to caries attack is self evident. The sensitivity of dentine and perception of pain can vary from person to person so, particularly for certain age groups, regular visits to a dentist are necessary. Eating habits and tooth care can also be seen as significant factors. Attacks of caries caught early can be dealt with by simple fillings that leave the pulp in place. In this case the pulp continues to replace dentine and the tooth stays 'alive'. If the stage of an abscess is reached then the administration of an antibiotic, followed by root canal treatment may save the tooth, though the pulp will no longer be able to fulfil its function of replacing dentine; the tooth is basically 'dead'. Drilling into the pulp chamber is another way of relieving the pressure and is an alternative treatment that is also likely to be followed by root canal treatment. In many cases an alveolar abscess leads to the loss of the tooth. When this problem occurs it is generally known as 'having an abscess' and patients sometimes go to a doctor rather than a dentist. Readers will now realise that this is very much a dental problem.

Gingivitis, or disease of the gums, is the name given to the first stage of a range of diseases that come under the heading of periodontal disease. The term periodontal disease means disease of the supporting structures of the teeth. In general other, more serious, periodontal diseases start from gingivitis, though they may also be connected with other medical diseases such as diabetes. The name given to the most common advanced form of periodontal diseases is periodontitis. Records indicate that more than 80% of the adult population of the UK suffers from periodontal disease, at some level, at any given time.

Figure 6.3 shows the progressive stages of gingivitis leading to periodontitis. Stage 1 indicates the position of the site where gingivitis occurs. The starting point for gingivitis is the accumulation of plaque in the gingival crevice as shown in stage 2. To a large extent this build-up of plaque can be checked by careful and consistent brushing with a relatively new brush and a suitable paste. The personal cleaning of teeth, on its own, is still not a totally effective measure against the build up of plaque. Visits to a dentist to receive the treatment known as scaling and polishing are also needed on a regular basis.

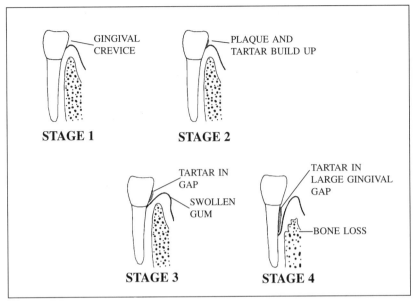

Figure 6.3

Gingivitis is encouraged by the build-up of tartar on the base of the teeth. Tartar is a hard stone-like substance that is formed in plaque over a period of time by saliva reacting with elements of plaque. If tartar forms in the gingival crevice the bacterial action within the surrounding plaque can start to intrude between the gum and the tooth. If this action is not halted then the next stage, known as chronic gingivitis, is seen as stage 3 in Figure 6.3. The gum is irritated by the foreign substances and becomes swollen, so losing its grip on the tooth allowing further intrusion of plaque and tartar. Another consequence at this stage is that the gum will ulcerate and start to bleed under pressure as when cleaning teeth. Such bleeding is often the first sign of more serious periodontal disease.

If the disease progresses to periodontitis as shown in stage 4 in Figure 6.3, the problem will need the careful attention of a dentist for the tooth not to be lost. Caries is the main cause of the loss of teeth in children and young adults, while periodontal disease is the major cause of lost teeth in older people. In general more teeth are lost through periodontal disease than caries.

As the formation of plaque is the main cause of gingivitis, one personal lesson to be taken from reading this chapter is that regular and efficient cleaning of teeth is likely to be the most effective way of inhibiting the start of gingivitis. Mouth rinses designed to remove plaque may also be helpful. Referring back to Figure 6.3, it is important to realise that home care, on its own, is not enough to keep periodontal disease under control. Regular visits to a dentist are necessary in order to make sure that any build up of plaque and tartar is dealt with at stage 2.

A major aim for this book is to enable readers to understand the nature and causes of the most common dental problems. If such understanding encourages some readers to modify their eating habits and ensure consistent care of teeth and gums for themselves and their children, then they will save themselves many £100s by savings in paying for treatment. This is in addition to time saved and perhaps most importantly, the saving of much pain and distress.

Chapter 7

Dental Records

and personal details
dentists need to know

Summary level

Everyone will need the services of a dentist at some time in their lives. Most people in the UK are registered with a dentist or a dental practice. Many people make regular visits at fixed intervals like every six months. All dental patients hope that their dentist will know about their dental history and any related problems they may have. On the other hand, dentists will have up to three thousand patients on their books and so need to keep some kind of record which will allow them to supply the kind of service that people expect. This chapter describes the records that are kept for individual patients, discusses the differences between front and back teeth, and gives details of the information that should be given to a dentist by a patient before that patient receives treatment.

Your dentist keeps a record of the state of your teeth on a 'chart' using codes as described in this chapter. Teeth in different positions have different functions and different shapes and individual teeth are identified by a coded description like 'Upper right 6'. In this chapter this way of keeping records is then used to discuss in more detail the different types of teeth and the functions they perform. Problems with the teeth and the mouth can interact with other medical conditions you may have, and records for these also have to be kept by your dentist.

Detailed level

Figure 7.1 is a diagrammatic representation of the teeth that is commonly used for recording purposes by dentists. This diagram is marked with a code that details the state of individual teeth, including treatments completed and problems that need attention. It may also be of interest that this record is used when bodies are identified by 'dental records'.

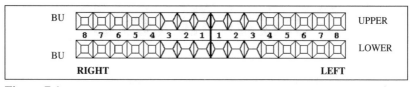

Figure 7.1

This chart as in Figure 7.1 is a part of NHS form FP25. It is recommended that dentists complete this form for every NHS dental patient. On a first visit to a new dentist this diagram will be filled in by an assistant responding to the dentist calling out the details of the teeth one by one. The diagram is marked by a code which indicates the nature of treatment previously completed or problems that need treatment. The basics of this code will be described in this chapter. The process of completing this diagram for an individual patient is known as charting.

For the purposes of this book, particular features of this diagram will be helpful in identifying the different types of teeth present in a full adult set. There are 32 teeth in a full set of upper and lower teeth. The 16 on the upper set and the 16 on the lower set are virtually mirror images of each other. In Figure 7.1 each tooth is represented by a square. In order to be able to provide a unique identification for each tooth they are numbered starting from the front. Along with this number, teeth are categorised as upper or lower and left or right side of the patient's mouth. So a tooth can be uniquely identified as 'Upper right 6'. The reader might like to note which square this identification gives in Figure 7.1.

Another feature of Figure 7.1 is that there are two different patterns within the squares that represent teeth. All the teeth numbered 1,2 and 3 have a different pattern to those numbered from 4 to 8. One of these patterns divides each tooth into four sections and the other into five sections. This difference in pattern arises because front and back teeth have a different anatomy and function and therefore a different shape. The front teeth in positions 1,2 and 3 are used for biting and have a top cutting edge. The back teeth, numbered 4 to 8, are used for chewing and have a cusp. A cusp is a hollowed out section in the centre of the top of the tooth.

In order to understand the idea behind dividing the square representing each tooth in Figure 7.1 into four or five sections, it will be helpful to look at a Figure 7.2, which is a pictorial representation of a lower set of teeth.

In Figure 7.2 the six teeth numbered 1,2 and 3 on each side are called the central incisor, the lateral incisor and the canine respectively. These six teeth are also known as front teeth and are the teeth used for biting. The other ten teeth, called the back teeth, are named individually as either the premolars or molars and are used for chewing. Each of the front teeth are represented by four surfaces in Figure 7.1. These surfaces are the front, the back and the sides

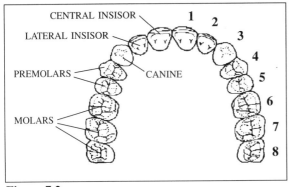

Figure 7.2

facing each of the next-door teeth. The back teeth have the extra surface at the top.

In dentistry the distinct surfaces of teeth (or sections of the squares in Figure 7.1) are identified by formal names and it is these names that are used when a dentist calls out the details to be recorded in Figure 7.1. One example of these formal names is 'buccal', so that if the dentist said 'Cavity in upper right 6 buccal', the assistant would then make the mark for a cavity in the relevant section of the identified square in Figure 7.1. One name for the outer surface of teeth that is in contact with either the cheeks or the lips, is the buccal surface. In figure 7.1 buccal surfaces are represented by the top row of spaces for the upper teeth and the bottom row for the lower teeth. The relevant rows of sections of teeth are labelled 'bu' in Figure 7.1. The reader might like to identify which space would be marked in Figure 7.1 for 'Upper right 6 buccal'.

While there is certainly no need for dental patients to know all the formal names for each surface, there may be some readers who are interested in such detail. The full selection of names plus a selection of the codes used to represent fillings, cavities etc. are given next. The codes are also useful as another indication of the different kinds of problems that can arise.

For the front teeth there are four surfaces to name. The front or outer surface has already been named as the buccal surface. While many dentists use this name for all front surfaces, there is another name for this surface for the front teeth only. In this case the surface can be called the labial surface. The distinction arises because buccal refers to cheeks and labial refers to lips. The back or inner surface has a different name for the upper and lower set of teeth. For the upper set this surface is called the palatal surface, for the lower set this surface is called the lingual surface. The other two surfaces are those facing other teeth. Both of these surfaces are known as proximal surfaces. The forward facing proximal surface of a tooth is known as the mesial surface and the backward facing proximal surface is known as the distal surface. An old filling might then be registered by a dentist to an assistant as 'Filling in lower left 3 distal'.

For the back teeth there is the extra surface which is known as the occlusal surface. The word occlusion in dentistry is significant because it means the positions of the teeth when the bottom set and top set meet. A dentist will talk about 'the occlusion'. Your occlusion has to be correct otherwise biting and chewing can be inefficient. A poor occlusion can also contribute to caries (tooth decay). The name occlusal surface for this section of back teeth follows naturally. For front teeth, it is the biting edges that have to occlude efficiently. These edges are sometime known as the incisal surface. This surface does not feature in Figure 7.1, as any problem which might affect this edge will also be present in either or both of the buccal and palatal/lingual surface.

Some of the most common codes for charting the condition and problems for teeth on Figure 7.1 are shown below:-

Another way of giving information in Figure 7.1 is to write initials as codes underneath the squares for relevant teeth. One common example is 'UE' which stands for 'Unerupted', meaning that the tooth has not yet appeared. This is very common for teeth numbered 8, as these are 'wisdom' teeth.

Now that the codes have been given it is possible to show examples of the way they are used. Figure 7.3 is used to illustrate how the codes are used for charting. The three examples represented are:-

(1) Cavity in upper right 6 buccal
(2) Filling in lower left 3 distal
(3) Upper left 8 extracted

Figure 7.3 shows how the three examples given are represented on this chart. It can be seen that charting provides a very concise way of recording detailed information. The chart can be used to record other information. One example is dentists checking for gingivitis and associated treatment planning by recording the depth of the gingival crevice at the front and back of each tooth.

There are two other major aspects to dental record-keeping. The first of these is a record of diagnosis and treatment for each occasion that a patient visits.

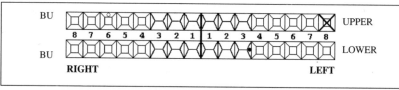

Figure 7.3

This record is similar to the record that doctors make for each patient visit.

The second aspect of dental record-keeping is making notes on the general medical condition of a patient. There are two kinds of medical information that everybody needs to give to their dentist. The first kind is for the dental record. For new patients in a practice a note needs to be made of their general state of health in as far as this might affect dental health and treatment. Such information will be recorded when you start with a new dental practice and needs to be updated as necessary. The second kind of information is concerned with medical conditions or treatments of a temporary nature, such as flu or receiving antibiotics for an infection. This second kind of information should be notified when making an appointment and/or when visiting your dentist while affected by the condition or treatment.

When you start with a new dental practice you will normally be asked about your general medical condition as a part of filling in your record. Some practices give new patients 'tick' lists to complete, and in others a dentist will discuss your general health and include specific questions as a part of the discussion. It is very important that a new dentist should know about any health problems you have; one way of dealing with this is to think about any visits you have made to a doctor in the last three years and then tell the dentist what the visits were for.

There are some medical conditions and treatments that are especially important to note on your dental record. A selection of these is given next in case it might help particular readers. It must be emphasised, however, that not all possibilities are covered. In a small book like this it is not possible to cover every eventuality, and the authors disclaim any responsibility for omissions that may affect particular cases; it is important that readers should tell dentists about any health problems they have, including mental illness. Given this disclaimer, some of the most important medical conditions and treatments that need to be reported to your dentist are: any heart, chest or breathing problems, including rheumatic fever; any ongoing medical treatment you are receiving such as drugs, or steroids, or irradiation; any allergies you have including allergies to drugs, or to local anaesthetics, or to sticking plaster; any bleeding disorders including a general difficulty in stopping bleeding; any known specific medical disease you have including cancer, diabetes, syphilis, hepatitis and HIV; any current known symptoms such as anaemia, high blood pressure or jaundice.

As an ongoing process, your dentist should also be told of any temporary medical conditions you may have and treatments you are receiving. Pregnancy and contact with particular infectious diseases, like mumps and German measles are particularly important. Dentists vary in whether they are willing to treat patients with respiratory problems encountered with colds, etc. It is always sensible to check with the receptionist.

Chapter 8

The patient experience

anaesthetics, instruments and X-rays

Summary level

The major purpose of this chapter is to allow readers to become aware of the main features of basic treatment in a dental surgery. Some readers may like to know details of what the dentist and dental assistant are doing, what the injections consist of, and how dental X-rays work; many such readers may then feel more relaxed because they are more knowledgeable about what is happening. Other readers will not want to know and they can pass over the detailed level of this chapter.

The chapter discusses three aspects of dental treatment that are common to all of the treatments that will be dealt with in the next seven chapters. The three aspects are (1) the use of anaesthetics (2) the nature and application of instruments for working on teeth (3) the use of X-rays for diagnosis.

Anaesthetics are used for a large proportion of dental work. Patients sometimes have a choice of whether to have an anaesthetic by injection or not. General anaesthetics are also sometimes used in dentistry. This chapter contains a description of how anaesthetics work and why there are three main types of injections for the local anaesthetics used in dentistry.

Instruments used for treatments in a dental surgery include hand tools and those needing an external power source. This chapter gives an overview of the way that a dental surgery functions in terms of what instruments are used, how they are used and whether the dentist or the dental assistant generally uses them.

Four different types of the application of X-rays for diagnosis and treatment within dentistry are also described in this chapter. The details given in this chapter are particularly useful for understanding what can happen in the course of treatment in a dental surgery and what a patient should expect and the precautions they should take in the hours immediately following treatment.

Detailed level
Anaesthetics

The purpose of anaesthetics is to stop pain messages going to the brain. In the case of dental treatment, anaesthetics will be administered for two main reasons. The first reason is to stop the patient from feeling pain and associated stress. The second reason is to allow the dentist to work without interruption by a patient who is suffering severe pain symptoms. People vary considerably in the way they react to pain from teeth. Some patients have high pain thresholds and prefer not to have anaesthetics. The choice of whether an anaesthetic should be administered for a particular treatment should be discussed at an early stage of an appointment.

Pain messages arrive at the brain through the complex system of nerves that supply the body. This system can be compared to the rooting system of a tree, with the comparatively large nerves that start from the brain branching out at various levels to finish with individual branches serving the nerve ends in an individual tooth or the front or back of the gum of a tooth. Figure 8.1 illustrates this branching structure.

The branching structure for the nerves which supply the teeth and gums start with a nerve known as the fifth cranial nerve. There is one of these for each side of the head. These nerves then divide into three branches, two of which supply the mouth area. These two are: (i) the maxillary nerve, which supplies the upper jaw and face, including the teeth and gums; (ii) the mandibular nerve, which supplies the lower part of the face, including the teeth and gums.

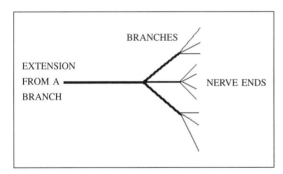

Figure 8.1

The maxillary nerve has five branches and the mandibular nerve has four branches. Each of these nine branches then subdivides again in order to serve individual teeth and other parts of the face such as the tongue, cheeks and sections of gum tissue. This is a very complex structure where an individual tooth will have one final branch of the nerve system leading to the nerve end in the pulp chamber, but the front and back of gums are often served by other nerve endings from different branches, starting a long way back from the individual tooth.

Local anaesthetics work on an individual nerve by blocking the pain messages being transmitted along that nerve. A suitable drug has to be injected as close as possible to the nerve. Drugs commonly used for this purpose in dentistry are Lignocaine or Prilocaine. Also included in the injection is a small amount of adrenaline which has a vasoconstrictor action which means that it makes the blood vessels contract in that area. The purpose of adding adrenaline is therefore to stop the other part of the drug leaving the area quickly through the natural function of the blood supply system. It keeps the contents of the injection in place for an hour or more. Adrenaline should not be used if the patient has heart disease or high blood pressure. There is an alternative for such patients. Injection materials arrive at the dentists in sealed capsules which, together with a disposable needle, are inserted into a device called a hypodermic syringe holder, which has a plunger to push the injection liquid from the capsule and through the needle. Both the capsule and needle are discarded immediately after use on an individual patient.

There are three types of local injections commonly used in dentistry. Some treatments will need just one of these types, others will need two. The three types are known as nerve block, local infiltration and intra-ligamentry injections. Some dentists will rub a surface anaesthetic onto the skin before giving injections in order to reduce pain from the insertion of the needle.

In the branching system of nerves for the teeth and gums there are places where the nerve system can be reached before a large part of the branching takes place. A **nerve block** is injected at the site of such places. A nerve block will therefore anaesthetise a range of teeth and gums. This type of injection is used mainly for back teeth on the lower jaw. A nerve block injection also affects the lips and surface of the mouth. Many readers will recognise these symptoms. It is important after such an injection to be careful with hot drinks and eating until the adrenaline has stopped being effective and sensation has returned. This injection requires a long needle to be fitted to the hypodermic syringe holder.

A **local infiltration** is given to block the messages from the solitary branch or nerve ending which enters a tooth or a gum. For an individual tooth the injection is given through the membrane at the base of the tooth as close to the apex as possible. the injection material has to soak through the supporting bone in order to work on the nerve. A short needle is used for this injection. This type of injection is not effective for the molars in the lower jaw because of the density of the supporting bone in this area.

Another way of anaesthetising an individual tooth and associated gums is to inject down the gingival crevice on each side of the tooth. Such injections are known as **intra-ligamentry injections**. This injection only affects the individual tooth and does not have the after-effects of a nerve block. It is given with a very short and differently-angled needle and also needs a special smaller cartridge of anaesthetic material. This injection is often used for molars on the lower jaw in adults and for all teeth in children.

It is possible to have a general anaesthetic for dental treatment. If this general anaesthetic is given in a dental surgery then it must be administered by an operator other than the dentist who is carrying out the treatment. Not many dentists now offer a general anaesthetic and patients who require one are referred to practices which do offer this service. A general anaesthetic is necessary when the work is extensive, like the extraction of a misplaced wisdom tooth, and is likely to last a long time. Such work is very often done in the dental wing of a hospital. The use of a general anaesthetic in a local dental surgery is mostly confined to patients (maybe children) who have a considerable fear of local injections and the following treatment when they are conscious.

One of the newer treatments being introduced into dental practices is a replacement for injections. This replacement is known as 'electronic anaesthesia' and is described in Chapter 16.

Instruments

The instruments used in dentistry can be divided into two groups. The first group are connected to a power unit and the second group are just hand tools. The standard equipment and furniture in a modern dental surgery is designed to make treatment as hygienic, quick and efficient as possible.

The central feature for the patient is still known as the dentist's 'chair', but the patient can easily be arranged at different heights and angles, with the chair being adjustable using power controls. Most treatment now is given with the patient in a horizontal position. The dentist and dental assistant have seats on either side of the patient which are adjustable for height. Situated next to the dentist is the delivery unit. Powered instruments are connected to this unit by retractable cables. These instruments are divided into two groups with each group having a different function. The first group is attached to the unit at the right of the patient and can only be used by a qualified dentist or dental hygienist. This group is concerned with delivery to the patient. Examples are drilling and syringing. The second set is concerned with collecting material from the patient for example a saliva ejector. These collection instruments are connected to the unit on the left of the patient and can be used by the dental assistant or the dentist. This description of the power unit applies to the majority in use, although some power units are set up differently.

The instruments are powered by compressed air generated by a compressor usually situated in another room. The principle is much the same as a vacuum cleaner. The instruments are designed to clip on the end of the cables. This means that there can be a very wide range of instruments available for use. New instruments are being developed all the time. Six of these instruments will be described in this section. The names of these six instruments are: airotor, handpiece, sonic scaler, three-way syringe, saliva ejector and aspirator. The first four of these are for delivery, the second two for collection. Airotors and handpieces are similar in many respect but are used for different tasks. Both airotors and handpieces are much the same size as a fat pen or pencil and they come in various shapes. One airotor in common use is illustrated in Figure 8.2.

Airotors are used by dentists to work on the hard surfaces of teeth or old

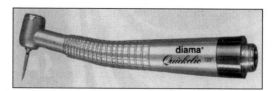

Figure 8.2

fillings in order to prepare for fillings, crowns etc. Looking at Figure 8.2, the right hand end clips on to the retractable cable and a 'bur' which rotates in order to remove enamel or filling fits into the centre of the curved section of the left hand end. There are many shapes of burs designed to fulfil different functions, some to remove and some to shape enamel, for example. Airotors make the burs rotate at very high speeds of up to 400,000 revolutions a minute. They have to be used with a built-in water spray in order to counteract the heat produced by the high-speed cutting. While these high speed airotors are very good at removing tissue quickly, they are also very safe to use, as it is not possible to exert pressure with them. The dentist has to stroke the surface rather than drill into it. The principle of handpieces and airotors is similar to a power drill used in the house, but the idea of drilling is not really appropriate in most dental work, even though the public perception is still of a dentist's drill. Airotors make a high-pitched whistling noise. The official name for an airotor is an 'airotor handpiece', but they are generally known just as 'airotors' and the name 'handpiece' is used for a similar tool which rotates much less quickly. These slower speed handpieces are used for the removal of softer substances like dentine. They are slightly more noisy than airotors and the sound is more like using a drill. A sonic scaler is a similar instrument but with a very small oscillating blade rather than a rotating bur. This instrument is used for the removal of tartar deposits as the first stage in the scaling and polishing of teeth. A water spray is attached to this device in order to cool and wash the teeth. The other main delivery powered instrument is the three-way syringe. It is called 'three-way' because it can deliver either a blast of air, a jet of water or a water spray, the last being a mixture of the first two.

Some dental practices are introducing new and different power instruments for cavity preparation etc. These are described in Chapter 16.

The two main collection powered instruments are the aspirator and saliva ejector. The aspirator is designed to collect material coming from the operation of an airotor or handpiece on a patient's tooth. The mouth of the aspirator has to be held in close proximity to the working head of the handpiece and nearly all the debris produced should then be removed immediately. In many dental practices it is the dental assistant who uses the aspirator, while the dentist uses the handpiece. Dental treatment these days is sometimes described as a 'four-handed' process because dental assistants are used more in actual treatment. A saliva ejector is fitted with a fan shaped end that stays in the patient's mouth while treatment is under way and removes saliva as it appears. This operation together with the use of cotton wool rolls etc. are designed to keep the working area dry.

Hand tools can be made of metal or plastic, depending on their function. They are used for various activities which include: (i) aids in diagnosis, such as mirrors and probes (ii) trimming and excavating enamel and dentine, such as metal chisels and scoops (iii) packing and trimming filling material, which are usually plastic or have replaceable plastic ends.

Plastic materials have the additional benefit that they can be discarded after use with an individual patient. All metal tools, including airotors and handpieces, have to be sterilised before use on another patient.

X-rays

The official name for the use of X-rays is radiography. Radiography works by placing film behind the area to be examined and passing X-rays through the lips, bone, teeth and gums of the exposed area. The principle behind radiography is that harder substances absorb X-rays and so show up as lighter areas on the exposed film. It is not easy to 'read' exposed radiography film. Interpreting the patterns of darker and lighter areas in order to draw conclusions needs considerable training and experience. The main use of radiography in dentistry is for diagnosis. Detecting the presence, size and nature of an abscess, locating the positions of roots and unerupted teeth or looking for bone loss and early development of caries.

The two types of radiography commonly used in dental practice are 'intra-oral' and 'extra-oral'. For intra-oral radiography the film is placed inside the mouth. One type of intra-oral film is positioned by the dentist and held in place over the teeth by the patient using a finger. This type of film is mainly used for checking on the condition of an individual tooth. Another type of intra-oral film is called 'bite wing', which is designed to check on teeth in occlusion i.e. when the upper and lower teeth are fitting together. This type of intra-oral radiography is used to check for caries at contact points of individual teeth. Bite wing film is positioned by the dentist and held in position by the bite of the teeth. In general, intra-oral radiography is designed to be used for a small range of teeth. The standard size of film is 3 cms by 4 cms.

Extra-oral film is designed to cover a larger area and is placed against the face outside the area of the mouth to be investigated. The film is held in place by a special holder. The experience for a patient is similar to receiving an X-ray in hospital.

There is a relatively recent method of generating a panoramic X-ray view of a patient's head, which includes the teeth. This is carried out with a machine called an orthopantomograph, usually known as an OPG. The patient sits inside a hood which then rotates around their head. Hospitals and some large dental practices are most likely to possess one of these machines.

Chapter 9

Fillings

amalgam and alternatives

Summary level

This chapter is concerned with the processes involved in diagnosis and treatment when the treatment includes a filling. In some ways the content of this chapter will be relevant to all readers because almost everybody has fillings in one or more teeth.

Although fillings are basically a common and standard treatment, on some occasions readers may have a choice of procedures and materials. In very rare and extreme cases these choices can severely affect a person's health. In other more common instances the choice could mean that the nature of filling or the material used might not necessarily be the best solution for the long term. The choices involved also frequently have financial implications. Dentists will usually give patients a chance to be involved in such choices. When such choice is offered it can be when patients are lying on a treatment couch, possibly with their mouths frozen up and with a gaping hole in a tooth. Not the best time for rational decision-making.

The detailed level section of this chapter is quite extensive but could give some readers vital information about the choices available. Other readers may think that as fillings are such a common treatment they do not need to read the detailed level in this chapter.

Fillings are used as a treatment for 'repairing' teeth when they are damaged (usually by caries). Fillings can only be used as a treatment if enough of the crown is left to form a secure structure for holding a filling in place. Fillings can vary considerably in complexity and in how difficult they are to complete and therefore how much they cost. This variation is dealt with in dentistry by arranging types of filling into different groups. The basis for the selection for each group is given in this chapter.

The outline procedure pattern for treatment by filling is:-

Start → Make the diagnosis → Consult with the patient → Give anaesthetic → Prepare the cavity → Line the cavity → Insert and trim the filling → Check occlusion → Harden filling → Finish

Choices for patients are mostly concerned with the type of material used for the filling and this chapter gives details, including advantages and disadvantages, in relation to four of the main materials used for fillings. Fillings should last for at least five years and can last for much longer, but can also fail prematurely for various specific reasons. Some of the reasons for failure are associated with the installation of the filling and others are to do with subsequent care by the patient and the dentist.

The detailed level in this chapter explains in some depth the requirements necessary for successful fillings and discusses other factors that help to produce a long-lasting filling. The question of costs for fillings can be complex because of the nature of choices and what is allowable under the NHS. Costs for fillings and associated treatment are given at the end of the chapter.

Different methods of filling holes in teeth are starting to be introduced in some dental practices, the details are in Chapter 16. Question 1 in Chapter 4 is about fillings. There are no case studies involving fillings.

Detailed level

Even though there is a lot of detail in this chapter, it is not possible to cover every eventuality for different types of filling and nature of materials. The aim has been to cover at least 90% of cases. Individual dentists also have their own preferences for materials and treatments, so possibilities that are described as normal in this chapter may not be recommended, or even available, at particular dental practices.

This chapter is broken down into four separate sections.

❖ General points about fillings
❖ Twelve factors needed for a successful filling
❖ Procedures and materials
❖ Financial considerations

The four sections are designed to be read in order. The financial implications, in particular, cannot be fully understood unless parts of the other sections have been assimilated to some degree. Some details are covered in more than one section in different degrees of detail. As an example, a rough guide to materials used for fillings is given in the requirements section, the nature and properties of the materials is covered in detail in the next section and the cost implications of choice of materials is given in the financial section.

General points about fillings

As a first point it is sensible to establish when filling is used as a treatment. Figure 9.1 shows a cavity in a tooth. Apart from the cut-out, which represents the cavity, it is a repeat of Figure 6.1 which was used to show the general structure of a tooth.

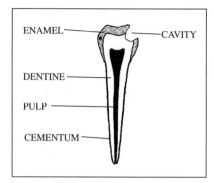

ENAMEL
CAVITY
DENTINE
PULP
CEMENTUM

Figure 9.1

In general such cavities are treated by filling. In Figure 9.1 the cavity is shown as having reached and affected the dentine that underlies the enamel, but has not yet affected the pulp chamber. In this case the cavity can still be treated with a filling. If the pulp chamber has been affected and pulpitis is present, then the pulpitis has to be treated as a first priority, but then can sometimes be followed by a filling.

Having established when filling is the appropriate treatment the next step is to consider the differences in the positions and types of cavity and the fillings that are used in each case. The dental profession has established a way of classifying fillings. This classification is based, to some extent, on the difficulty of completing the filling so it has a bearing on cost. The classification will be used later in this chapter to indicate when different procedures have to be followed.

The five classes of fillings are defined as follows:-

Class I fillings are those that involve a single surface. Two possible cases of Class I fillings are illustrated in Figure 9.2, which shows how Class I fillings for individual teeth are represented on the chart kept as a dental record.

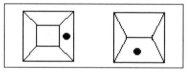

Figure 9.2

Class II fillings are those that involve two or more surfaces of back teeth. Figure 9.3 illustrates two possible cases of Class II fillings. Such fillings are described by the initials of the surfaces they cross. The three possibilities are DO, MO and MOD which stand for Distal Occlusal, Mesial Occlusal and Mesial Occlusal Distal respectively.

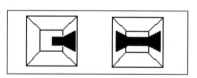

Figure 9.3

Class III fillings are those carried out on the surfaces of front teeth that are adjacent to the next tooth. The names of these surfaces are mesial or distal, so a

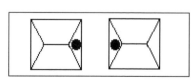

Figure 9.4

Class III filling is on the mesial or distal surface of a front tooth. This is illustrated in Figure 9.4.

Class IV fillings are an extension of class III fillings in that the filling extends to the incisal or cutting edge of the tooth.

Class V fillings are those where the filling has to be made next to, or even partly below, the gum. In technical terms this is at the cervical margin of the tooth.

In general a filling should remain viable for between 3 and 20 years. Another reason for giving the list of factors required for fillings, which forms the next section of this chapter, is that it gives an indication of ways in which fillings might fail. Complete eradication of all these factors, for every filling they undertake, is impossible for any dentist. If a dentist takes more time and uses more expensive equipment on occasions, this can increase the likelihood of fillings staying viable for longer periods of time. Private treatment is thus more likely to provide these extra benefits. One factor that has been shown to help in the duration of fillings is a patient/dentist relationship that has lasted a long time. Patients who switch dentists regularly tend to have more problems with fillings that fail prematurely.

Twelve factors needed for a successful filling
In some ways filling may seem a very simple procedure as it is just a plug for a hole in a tooth. In fact there are many requirements that have to be satisfied for a filling to be a successful, long-lasting, replacement for the natural material of a tooth. The process and nature of the treatment, coupled with problems associated with dealing with a wide variety of patients successfully in a restricted period of time, brings in other complications.

In this section twelve factors needed for a successful filling are identified. Each of these factors has a brief statement outlining the basic facts, which is then followed by an amplification for readers who require more detail.

Factor 1 The filling has to be hard wearing, rigid and immovable.
These properties are governed by the material used for the filling and the way that it is held in the cavity. There are four basic materials used for permanent fillings: silver amalgam, composite resin, glass ionomer cement and gold. These are fixed in the cavity either mechanically, or chemically or by a mixture of the two. The nature, properties and way of fixing these four materials will be discussed in detail in the next section. At this stage it will be useful to look at what is meant by a mechanical way of holding a filling in place and then to contrast it with chemical ways of retaining fillings.

A mechanical method of securing a filling applies when the filling is inserted as a soft material and is then made to harden. The black section in Figure 9.5

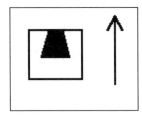

Figure 9.5

indicates the position of the filling material. In order for the filling not to move in the direction of the arrow the cavity has to be prepared so that the filling is wider at the base. When the filling hardens it will then be physically fixed. The principle is the same as making a dovetail joint in woodwork. For Class II fillings there are two possible ways in which the filling could slip. For Class II fillings the arrangement shown in Figure 9.5 has to apply both vertically and laterally.

Fillings are fixed chemically either by the use an adhesive or by having a filling material that adheres to the natural materials present in teeth.

Factor 2 The filling should be the same size and shape as the original, especially with regard to occlusion.

This factor seems obvious, but achieving this exact match does raise another set of problems. As stated in an earlier chapter, a poor occlusion resulting from a filling can leave places for plaque to accumulate, leading to possible further caries attack. In general fillings are inserted as soft materials and then either start to harden with time or are treated in order to harden them. When the material is soft it can easily be manipulated, but when it is hard it will need abrasive treatment in order to change its shape. This generally means using an airotor (see Chapter 8).

Another problem with using an abrasive after the filling has hardened is that too much filling can be removed. As this lost filling cannot then easily be replaced, the result will be a space where plaque can accumulate. In order to test occlusion the dentist will need to ask the patient to 'bite'. If the filling material is too soft at this stage then distortion can take place. Methods of fulfilling Factor 2 will be discussed in more detail under the headings of different filling materials.

Factor 3 The filling should not irritate dentine or pulp and should not conduct heat.

If some filling materials have direct contact with dentine they act as a chemical irritant which results in pain and eventual break down of the dentine. If such materials are used for fillings then they must be separated from the dentine by the insertion of a lining for the cavity before the insertion of the filling. In fact all fillings are placed over a lining. When silver amalgam or gold (both 'metals') are used then the lining also has to act as an insulator to protect the dentine from extremes of hot and cold. Linings can also perform an adhesive function. The range of materials used for linings will be discussed in detail in the next section on materials.

Factor 4 The filling should not expand or contract, especially at the margins.

The nature of the filling material is the main factor here. These days, nearly all dentists use filling materials that come ready-mixed. If mixing has to be done just before filling, this can result in slight mistakes in ratios of filling material to hardening material, and/or tiny air bubbles left in the resulting mix. The process of placing the filling in the cavity is also important. Any spaces left, however small, will result in shrinkage eventually. It is at the margins of a filling where any shrinkage is likely to show itself. These gaps represent an obvious place for breakdown. Preparation of cavities needs special attention at the margins. The filling must have a smooth fit and must not contract with time.

Factor 5 The filling must affect appearance as little as possible.

With present dental technology it is possible to match any shade of tooth colour very precisely. It is also possible to apply external coating material where teeth have become discoloured. The filling material that allows this close matching is composite resin, so this material is generally used for front teeth. Silver amalgam and gold both contrast strongly with any shade of white and so are generally used only for back teeth. Composite resin can also be used for back teeth. There are other factors that relate to choice besides colour matching. These factors will be dealt with in the next section.

Factor 6 The filling must be able to be fixed quickly.

There are several different factors in relation to time. The dentist needs some time to place and shape the filling, but filling material that took three days to set hard would obviously be impractical. Silver amalgam does take several hours to set completely, so if it is used for a filling the patient should be advised not to eat on that side for the rest of the day. The way that composite resins are hardened will be discussed in detail in the next section, but generally teeth filled with these can be used immediately.

Factor 7 All diseased tissue must be removed.

Fillings are generally used as a treatment after a tooth has suffered from caries attack. It often happens that the visible surface cavity for a caries attack is small, but the underlying damage to dentine is considerable. On a dental visit where filling is the eventual treatment, the dentist will often not know the full extent of the attack until the cavity is opened up for inspection. Consequent treatment must include removal of all diseased tissue. Any diseased tissue left will be a prime source of failure for the filling.

Factor 8 Any unsupported enamel must be removed.

As stated earlier, enamel is the hardest substance in the body, but if left unsupported it can fracture. Cavity preparation has to ensure that the enamel left on the tooth is adequately supported. At the same time enamel left on the tooth must be shaped so that the margin with the filling is smooth.

Factor 9 Any moisture left in a cavity when filling or lining material is applied will be a potential cause of failure.

Both lining and filling materials have to be applied to a totally dry surface. As the interior of a mouth is a very moist area, this dry condition can be difficult to achieve. Various ways of keeping the cavity dry are employed such as: aspirators, saliva ejectors, cotton or rubber pads inserted to isolate the tooth undergoing treatment, small pads wiped on the inside of the cavity and blasts of air from a syringe. The timing between the final drying out of the cavity and the insertion of the lining and filling is crucial. It usually needs the dentist and assistant to work closely together in order to keep any delay to a minimum.

Factor 10 The patient should suffer as little pain, shock or strain as possible.

Many aspects of receiving filling as a treatment can cause pain, shock or strain. The use of airotors or handpieces, anaesthetic injections, keeping the mouth in a fixed open position for a long period of time, or even just the sounds and sights associated with dental treatment, are all factors that might affect patients. As part of the treatment a dentist will try to keep all of these factors to a minimum. Time is a very significant factor here. Keeping the time for treatment as short as possible is not trying to fit in more patients, but represents an attempt to lessen the strain on the patient. There is a difficult path to tread in taking as much care as possible without over-stretching the capacity of the patient to stay in a receptive state for treatment. The dentist and patient relationship is also important. The patient needs faith in the dentist and the dentist needs to be able to make a good estimate of the patient's attitude to pain and capacity for prolonged treatment. Another major purpose of this book is to give patients knowledge about what is happening to them. For many people such knowledge will help them to be calmer when undergoing treatment. It is important to realise that some degree of shock is always present. It is sensible to plan to relax after receiving filling as a treatment, rather than go straight back to work and decision-making.

Factor 11 Care has to be taken to guard against infection and problems from flying particles.

A filling is basically a minor operation. It involves using instruments which come into contact with tissue that can easily become infected. The mouth is a source of many bacteria and possible viruses, some of which can be harmful if passed on to others. Another potential source of danger is the use of an airotor or handpiece. The problem is that particles fly in all directions from the centre of activity. Some of these particles will contain infected material and some might contain amalgam. As discussed in detail in the next section, amalgam has mercury as one constituent so needs handling with care. The two major factors which ensure patient safety are as much use as possible of disposable equipment, and very careful sterilisation of instruments between the treatment of individual patients.

Factor 12 A correct initial diagnosis has to be made, although the diagnosis may have to change during treatment.

Fillings can vary in many ways including the size of the filling, the material to be used and the time the work will take. If the patient is in pain the place of filling early or late in the treatment must be considered. An incorrect initial diagnosis could result in unsuitable choices and subsequent early failure. One major factor is whether the pulp is affected and, if so, is the consequent pulpitis reversible or not. The patient can be of major help here, because the nature of the pain is a good indication of where disease has reached. If the pain brought on by hot and cold substances only lasts a short time (a few seconds to five minutes) then the pulpitis is probably reversible. If the pain lasts longer then the pulpitis is probably irreversible. If pain occurs without any external stimulus, then pulpitis will be well established and an abscess has probably either started to form or not be far away. Another help for diagnosis is an X-ray as described in Chapter 8. This diagnosis may change once all diseased tissue is removed, as the dentist may then see that the pulp chamber has been damaged.

Procedures and materials

Having established the factors necessary for a successful filling, it is now possible to discuss the procedures for installing fillings, and the materials used for fillings, at a reasonably detailed level. The aim in this section is to give enough detail for readers to make choices and have some understanding, without overloading them with too much information. The section basically describes the various different types of filling material available and the procedures for filling and lining associated with each type. Discussion of filling materials and linings have not been placed separately because in some ways the distinctions are blurred.

The outline procedure pattern for treatment by filling is:-

Start ➜ Make the diagnosis ➜ Consult with the patient ➜ Give anaesthetic
➜ Prepare the cavity ➜ Line the cavity ➜ Insert and trim the filling
➜ Check occlusion ➜ Harden filling ➜ Finish

This pattern can be interrupted by the need for the pulp to settle down before inserting a permanent filling. In these cases a temporary filling is used until a further appointment. Some lining materials are also used as temporary fillings or as adhesives for permanent fillings.

In general four materials are used for permanent fillings: silver amalgam, composite resin, glass ionomer cement and gold.

Silver amalgam or 'amalgam' as it is generally known, has been used for filling teeth for over a hundred years. In chemical terms it is a metal alloy. Metal alloys consist of mixtures of different metals, but the resulting alloy then acts as a distinct metal with properties of its own. Other well-known metal alloys are bronze and steel. Amalgam is an alloy of silver, tin, copper, zinc and mercury. Mercury is generally in liquid form at room temperatures. When added to the other ingredients to form amalgam the alloy is soft, but then solidifies with time. The hardening process for an amalgam filling is therefore built in and the mercury has to be mixed with the other ingredients just before the amalgam is used. In a dental surgery the assistant will prepare the amalgam in an instrument known as an amalgamator and then pass the amalgam to the dentist in an instrument called an amalgam carrier which allows the dentist to insert small quantities of amalgam at a time into a cavity.

As noted in Factor 1, when a filling is inserted in a soft form and then goes hard it has to be made to stay in place by mechanical means. As metals and metal alloys are very good heat conductors, deep amalgam fillings have to be lined in order to insulate the pulp against pain from hot and cold substances. Common linings used for such insulation are zinc phosphate or calcium hydroxide, which protect against heat but can be an irritant to dentine. Deep amalgam fillings therefore usually have two linings or a varnish and a lining. Amalgam starts to harden quite soon, so the dentist will be able to do some shaping by cutting but then may have to use an airotor in order to generate a correct occlusion.

Amalgam is very long-lasting, but the silver colour contrasts strongly with the white of teeth. This contrast in colour stops amalgam from use as a filling for front teeth but it is the most common choice as a filling for back teeth. When amalgam is used for class II fillings where the cavity extends to a side surface of a tooth, the filling process will also involve the use of a matrix band which is fitted round the tooth in order to retain the filling. A matrix band has a metal strip which is fitted round the tooth and then tightened with a screw. A household device which works in a similar way is a clamp for holding pipes onto taps. When the filling is complete the matrix band is removed.

It is likely that most readers will have at least one amalgam filling. They are relatively easy to install and last well. Mercury in liquid or vapour form is highly poisonous so the preparation of amalgam in the dental surgery is undertaken with great care. As previously stated, alloys have different properties from the metals which make the mix, and in amalgam the poisonous properties of the mercury are generally believed to be lost, although research has introduced slight doubts about this assumption. In relatively recent times there have been reported cases of people who react badly to amalgam fillings, even to the extent of not being able to lead normal lives. Replacing all amalgam fillings by composite resins has restored them to normal. Such cases are extremely rare, but in general it may not be sensible in the long term to place any material that contains a highly poisonous element in the mouth and an alternative material with the same properties as amalgam is likely to be developed. For new fillings it is now possible to choose either amalgam or composite resin for fillings on back teeth, so this is one area where the details in this book may help with decision making.

Composite resin fillings consist of a mix of materials which can be made to set hard by a chemical process. Such materials have many uses outside of dentistry. For filling dents in cars or DIY around the house for example. There is a wide range of composite fillings available for dental purposes. It is possible to match any colour of tooth, and to have composite resin fillings that are capable of withstanding the forces applied at the chewing surfaces of back teeth. Composite fillings have been made very easy to use, as they come in a ready-mixed soft form and are hardened by an intense beam of Ultra Violet light from a special lamp. The dentist can therefore carry out the total shaping and occlusion-forming process before the filling is hardened with the light treatment.

As composite resin fillings are inserted soft and then hardened they can be retained by the same mechanical process as amalgam fillings. There is also another way of retaining composite fillings on to enamel. This method is known as 'acid etching' and consists of painting the enamel with phosphoric acid for up to sixty seconds. When the acid is washed away the enamel is left with a surface honeycomb effect into which the composite resin can flow and make a permanent bond with the enamel. This method is particularly useful for front teeth, especially those that have been fractured in accidents. The method is also useful for fissure sealing. Fissures are the natural small holes in the chewing surfaces of back teeth. If they are sealed in this way it stops the fissure from becoming a site for the build up of plaque.

Unlike amalgam, composite resins are not good conductors of heat. They may irritate the pulp and so deep fillings need lining. The lining often consists of ready-mixed paste whose main ingredient is calcium hydroxide. This paste soothes dentine and pulp and is adhesive. It can also be made in order to release fluoride slowly into the tooth.

Composite resin is now the main material used for class III and class IV fillings for front teeth. With modern technology it is also possible for composite fillings to be used for back teeth. People now have a choice of having filled teeth that all match in colour and to avoid amalgam if they wish.

Early composite fillings tended to need replacement within five years, but this drawback has now largely been overcome.

Glass ionomer cement is a mixture of materials that include a glass-like substance and an acid which acts as a bonding agent. The main advantage of the filling is that it bonds naturally to enamel, dentine and cementum. It is also a non-irritant and so does not need a lining. The main disadvantage as a filling on its own is that it cannot withstand the forces required for chewing or biting. Glass ionomer cement is used on its own mainly for class V fillings, that is for cavities in teeth at the gum margin. Glass ionomer cement is also often used in conjunction with other materials as a lining or a first layer of filling.

Glass ionomer cement is mixed just before use and hardens quickly. The surface of the cavity must be totally dry and no shaping or polishing of the filling should take place until it has been in place for 24 hours. When this filling is used on its own it therefore requires different techniques which include holding with a plastic matrix, varnishing the surface immediately after first installation and a later visit for trimming and shaping.

Readers are only likely to be aware of receiving a glass ionomer filling if they have a class V cavity. Until recently these fillings were a natural dark shade of white, so did not match teeth colour precisely. It is now possible to make nearly as a good a match as composite. As glass ionomer adheres naturally to teeth and does not need much cavity preparation it is sometimes used for deciduous teeth. The lack of wearing ability is not such an important feature for these teeth.

Gold is the strongest of all filling materials, but gold fillings have to be made from a wax impression and then cemented into place. The cavity cannot then be undercut but has to be a U shape. Both from the time imposed by the extended nature of the treatment and the expense of the material and the manufacture of the filling from the impression, gold fillings are expensive. Gold fillings are an alternative to amalgam for back teeth. They are likely to last longer, but can still suffer from decay in the supporting structure of the tooth.

There are two other aspects of fillings that are fairly common and need discussion in this chapter. The first of these is the use of temporary fillings and the second aspect is the procedures available when the filling has to occupy a large space.

Temporary fillings are used on occasions when it is inappropriate to insert the permanent filling immediately. The factor causing the delay can be lack of time on a particular emergency appointment or a clinical reason like allowing the pulp to settle or waiting for a gold filling to be made. Temporary fillings also often have soothing and remedial properties. Temporary fillings are generated in the surgery either by mixing a propriety product on a slab or heating sections of pink or white sticks of a substance known as gutta percha. When these are heated they soften and can then be inserted into a cavity. Materials used for temporary fillings usually have other uses such as linings or first layers of a sectioned filling.

When a large amount of natural tooth material has to be replaced then there can be a choice of whether to use a filling or a crown. The use of artificial crowns is discussed in detail in the next chapter. One distinction for the patient between fillings and crowns is that artificial crowns are made at dental laboratories in between appointments, while fillings are applied by the dentist using materials as described above. If fillings are very extensive then they may need extra support and/or to be built up in layers of different materials. A common procedure for giving extra support is to make threaded holes in the dentine and to screw in tiny pins which are then integrated into the filling material. The principle is similar to concrete being reinforced with steel bars.

Table of costs

The pricing structure for fillings is relatively straightforward compared to some of the more complex dental treatments featured in later chapters. In general terms both with the NHS and privately the charge is likely to be per filling and the pricing structure is given in a table on the next page. There are three points about dental pricing which readers may find useful in addition to the details in the table:-

1. Under NHS regulations white composite fillings are not allowable on the occlusal surfaces of back teeth. This means that if a patient wants to choose composite rather than amalgam for back teeth then they will have to pay the private rate for such fillings.

2. If the filling is a part of a larger treatment, when it follows root canal treatment for example, then the bill will include all of the items. Checking the bill will need the patient to be able to list for themselves all the aspects of the treatment for which payments have to be made.

3. Following on from 2, it is common practice in dentistry not to give itemised bills. In private practice the bill is quite likely to say 'For dental treatment' and then give a total sum. In order to maintain some control over expenditure it is important to ask for estimates, even if in pain and thinking that paying any price is worth the relief.

In 1996, NHS dental patients who did not qualify for free treatment had to pay 80% of the cost, with a maximum of £300 for any one treatment. It is the amount that patients had to pay that is set out in the table. Dentists in private practice set their own charges. The private fees given in the table are taken from those suggested by the General Dental Practitioners Association. Some dentists (especially specialists) may well differ from these figures by a considerable margin. It should be remembered that fillings will almost certainly be preceded by examination, plus a possible X-ray, and the charges for these will be added to the bill received for a filling.

The table contains a range of possible charges for each treatment. The reasons for this range are evident from the details given previously in this chapter. Fillings may cover more than one surface of tooth and therefore be in a different class and cost more to complete, X-rays can be of different types, examinations can involve more time depending on whether it is a first appointment where the chart needs completion and other factors like the place and nature of the problem area.

The price ranges for private practice given by the General Dental Practitioners Association are divided into four groups. The reason for this division is that the overheads for dentists, like rent, staff salaries etc., will differ according to the site of the particular surgery. The charge per hour that a dentist makes for treatment is designed to cover these overheads as well as provide the dentist's own salary.

The scales are based on a notional charge per hour as follows:-

Scale I   £70 per hour
Scale II   £80 per hour
Scale III   £90 per hour
Scale IV   £100 per hour

Using the table and with knowledge gained from this book on what a particular treatment entails, readers should be able to generate an itemised account to give an overall total to compare with a final bill from a dentist. It should also be possible to work out a rough estimate of what the cost of a particular course of treatment might be for a member of the family.

The figures in the table are for 1996 and are approximate to the nearest £. The top figure in each space is the minimum level of charge and the bottom figure is the maximum. The minimum figure is for routine work and is therefore the most likely figure that will occur.

Treatment	NHS	I	II	III	IV
Examination	4	11	17	19	23
	12	33	51	57	69
X-ray	2	5	6	7	8
	4	10	12	14	16
Amalgam	4	11	14	19	27
filling	12	33	42	57	81
Composite	8	19	21	24	30
front filling	11	26	28	33	41
Composite	N/A	15	19	25	34
back filling		45	57	75	102
Fissure seal	4	11	14	19	27
	6	17	21	27	40
Glass ionomer	7	17	19	22	28
cement filling	10	24	27	31	39

Chapter 10

Saving natural teeth

with root canal treatment and crowns

Summary level

This chapter deals with a subject that is likely to affect most people at some time in their lives. This is because many teeth eventually reach a stage where they are causing problems because tooth decay has penetrated to the root at the centre of the tooth (see Figure 6.1). In such cases the treatments described in this chapter can be an alternative to extraction for the tooth concerned. It is also true that many teeth are extracted in dental surgeries that could have been left in place with root canal treatment and possibly an artificial crown fitted. It should be common for dental patients to be given a choice of root canal treatment or extraction for an individual tooth. Knowledge of the information given in this chapter will help patients considerably when it comes to discussing a choice of either extraction and replacement with an artificial tooth, or using root canal treatment in order to save the natural tooth.

Unlike Chapter 9 on fillings, it is essential that anyone who hopes that a tooth might be saved with root canal treatment should read the detailed level in this chapter. This is because the treatment is more involved and stands more chance of failure; readers should be as clear as possible about the consequences of choosing root canal filling and/or crowns as treatments.

The two treatments covered in this chapter are not necessarily used in conjunction. Root canal treatment and the use of artificial crowns appear as separate subjects in textbooks for dental students. The reason why they are put together in this chapter is because, if they are used either separately or in conjunction, they can give an alternative to extractions, bridges and dentures which are the treatments grouped together in Chapter 11.

The detailed level starts by discussing when crowns and root canal treatment are appropriate treatments. Looking at Figures 10.1, 10.2 and 10.3 will help readers to follow the explanation that follows next. An artificial crown is necessary if the natural crown has lost too much material to keep a filling in place (Figure 10.1). The purpose of root canal treatment is to remove diseased material from the pulp chamber and root canal (Figure 10.2) and replace it with inert filling material. If the natural crown is not viable and the root canal has to be filled then a post can be inserted in the root canal chamber in order to support an artificial crown (Figure 10.3). The complex nature of root canal treatment is described in the detailed level by dividing the procedures necessary for successful treatment into seven stages. The materials for artificial crowns and the procedures required to make and fit them are also described in detail.

At the end of the chapter there is a table giving costs for the treatments covered in this chapter. Question 2 in Chapter 4 is about root canal treatment. Case Study 9 in Chapter 5 involves root canal treatment and Case Studies 8 and 10 include the use of crowns.

Detailed level

Root canal treatment is a part of dentistry which comes under the heading of 'Endodontics'. There are endodontic specialists in dentistry in a similar way to specialists (like heart specialists) in medicine. In the UK most dental practices now offer root canal treatment, though this is a relatively recent development. For some other aspects of endodontic treatment patients might have to be referred to a specialist.

Before going into the details of root canal treatment and the use of artificial crowns it is sensible to establish when these treatments are used and the relationship between them. This will be done by diagrammatic representations of three theoretical cases with a short description to follow each diagram.

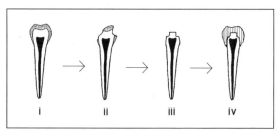

Figure 10.1

Figure 10.1 shows the progression from an undamaged tooth represented by stage (i) to stage (ii) where a caries attack has affected most of the enamel but not penetrated to the pulp so that pulpitis is not present. A filling is not possible because not enough of the crown is left in place. In this case the dentine can be shaped as in stage (iii) in order to provide a protrusion and shoulders onto which an artificial crown can be cemented as in stage (iv).

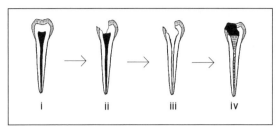

Figure 10.2

Figure 10.2 represents the progression from a normal sound tooth represented by stage (i) to stage (ii) where a caries attack has penetrated the enamel and dentine and also reached the pulp so that pulpitis has developed. Another difference to the first case is that much of the enamel and dentine is still intact, so that the crown can still be treated by filling rather than having to install an artificial crown. In this case stage (iii) shows the normal preparation for a filling in the crown, plus the root chamber and root canal which are both emptied and cleaned ready for filling. Stage (iv) shows the root canal filled with a normal filling also present in the crown.

It is this cleaning and filling of the root chamber and canal which is known as root canal treatment and that is a part of endodontics.

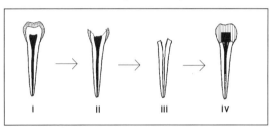

Figure 10.3

Figure 10.3 represents the progression from a sound tooth at stage (i) to stage (ii) where the tooth has lost most of the crown and is also affected by pulpitis. In this case most of the rest of the crown has to be removed and the root canal emptied and cleaned as in stage (iii). In order to be able to fix an artificial crown a metal post is cemented into the root canal. The rest of the root canal is filled and the crown is then attached using the metal post as an anchor. This final situation is shown as stage (iv) in Figure 10.3.

The three cases represented by Figures 10.1, 10.2 and 10.3 are all commonly available at dental practices. The root canal can also be approached and treated from the apex of the tooth rather than the crown. This treatment is known as apicectomy. It can be used when standard root canal treatment has failed or is not suitable. Apicectomy is discussed in Chapter 15.

Root canal treatment

Having established when root canal treatment and artificial crowns are normally used, this chapter continues with a detailed description of procedures and possibilities. Root canal treatment is dealt with first.

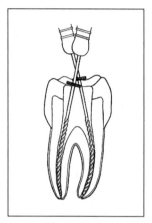

Figure 10.4

Figure 10.4 will be used in a detailed description of one aspect of root canal treatment. Figure 10.4 will also act as a general illustration that should help readers to visualise issues and problems that occur in root canal treatment. The purpose of root canal treatment is to remove irreversibly damaged pulp and to replace it with a filling that will seal the canal system. While this treatment may seem similar to ordinary fillings, there are additional features that cause difficulty. Figure 10.4 shows files that have penetrated two roots on a back tooth. Back teeth all have more than one root. Some of these roots can be misshapen and they can even join in some places. The entrance to a root canal from a pulp chamber can be difficult to find. Front teeth only have one root and so are usually easier to deal with by root canal treatment. All root canals are very narrow, ranging from 0.5mm to 2mm. The dentist can widen these canals with instruments, but has to take care not to divert from the path of the canal or to go beyond the apex of the tooth.

The procedures for carrying out a root canal filling will be listed as a sequence of seven stages. The detail for each stage will include ways in which the problems given above are overcome. After the list of procedures the implications for the patient will be discussed, together with the possible long term effects of receiving root canal treatment.

Root canal treatment – stage 1

Stage 1 is to gain access to the root canal (or canals) through the crown of the tooth. Very often this is a relatively simple procedure because the crown needs treatment in any case. On the other hand, there can be cases where root canal treatment is needed underneath a filling which does not need replacement. In this case the dentist will want to disturb this filling as little as possible. For back teeth, which can have as many as four root canals, gaining access can mean that a relatively large space has to be generated in order to locate the start of each root. The procedure for this stage is similar to preparation for a filling. The patient will usually have a local anaesthetic, the space is excavated using airotors, handpieces and hand tools. The diagnosis will often have been made with the use of an X-ray.

Root canal treatment – stage 2

Stage 2 is to locate the start of each root canal and to improve access if necessary. This stage is an extension of the first stage. Referring to Figure 10.4, it can be seen that instruments have to be passed down each root canal and then manipulated. The access to the canals therefore has to be widened sometimes. This procedure is done with a handpiece or hand tools designed for shaping dentine.

Root canal treatment – stage 3

Stage 3 is to use broaches, reamers and files to remove pulp and debris from the canals and then to enlarge the canals. Barbed broaches are rotated by hand. The barbs engage the pulp, which can then be withdrawn. Reamers and drills resemble wood drills and are used for enlarging and smoothing the canals. Both of these instruments are supplied in graded sizes so that the dentist can gradually increase the depth and width of the cleared space in a root canal. Figure 10.4 shows files present in the root canals. This procedure is not easy. The instruments have to be manipulated by hand very carefully. Referring to Figure 10.4, the part of the files at the top that look like flower buds are the part that the dentist holds between finger and thumb in order to manipulate the files. Care also has to be taken not to remove too much material or progress too far and so breach the apex of the canal. There are power instruments which can help with this stage.

Root canal treatment – stage 4

Stage 4 is to take an X-ray in order to check on the position of the end of the canals. As noted earlier, the whole canal has to be cleaned, but it is vital that the apical foramen is not breached. In technical terms at this stage, the dentist has to determine the 'working length' for a particular canal. Figure 10.4 demonstrates what the working length is and how it is determined. The procedure starts by placing a small plastic stop on a file. In Figure 10.4 these stops are represented by the two thick black lines at the top of the tooth. The file is then manipulated down the canal until the dentist reckons that the end is reasonably close to the end of the root. The stop is then adjusted to give a referral point on the cusp for a back tooth, or the incisal edge for a front tooth. When all these files are in place an X-ray is taken. For the patient the experience of moving to the X-ray machine from the dentist's chair with a mouthful of metal may seem rather strange. Readers will now know why it is done. If the X-rays show that the files have not penetrated enough, the procedure may have to be repeated. Normally, at this stage the dentist will estimate the working length as the distance between the stop and the end of the file. This working length could be 18.5mm for example. All subsequent operations on the root will be carried out using that working length.

Root canal treatment – stage 5

Stage 5 is to clean and dry the canals. After the working length has been established, some more work on extending and enlarging the canals might be needed. The canals are then irrigated by flushing with various solutions. This irrigation must be confined to the root canal. Liquid is usually injected and retrieved using a hypodermic syringe. The canals are then dried with commercially provided paper points, once again using the working length. Some patients receiving root canal treatment might receive a temporary filling at this stage, rather than the dentist continuing to the final result. This two-stage approach is most likely to happen when the tooth needs to heal before continuing with the permanent filling. Some dentists will always adopt this two stage approach as a precautionary measure.

Root canal treatment – stage 6

Stage 6 is to sterilise and line the canal. As with fillings a lining is inserted into the canal before the filling material. The purpose of the lining is to sterilise the canal and sometimes also to act as a cement for the filling as well. The lining is inserted by using a file with increasing amounts of lining material. The first small amount has to be placed using the working length.

Root canal treatment – stage 7

Stage 7 is to apply the filling to the canal. This stage might also involve the fitting of a post or posts if the tooth is to receive an artificial crown. The most common material for root canal filling is 'gutta percha'. This is an inert material which softens when heated. Gutta percha is inserted in the root using a special instrument which ensures that the whole canal is filled but not too much pressure is exerted. Other materials may also be used for filling root canals. Endodontics is an area where much research and innovation is taking place.

For the patient, this treatment is likely to last a long time and can be tiring. At the very least it will involve a half-hour visit to the dentist. Even for treating a single tooth, root canal treatment can take two or three long visits. Root-filled teeth are normally not a source of pain, but just occasionally they can feel sore for up to a week and some discomfort may continue for another week or two. A few people find that root canal filled teeth will continue to give occasional, relatively mild, discomfort. If pain becomes persistent and intense it could be that the treatment has failed and that disease is present again. The failure rate for root canal treatment is around 5% to 15%, depending on the position of the tooth and the nature of the procedures. Endodontics is an area of treatment where taking extra time and care, plus using more sophisticated and advanced equipment, can improve the chance of success. Such extras obviously have to be paid for. If a root canal treatment fails then it can sometimes be repeated or the canal can be approached from the apex (the treatment known as apicectomy referred to earlier) or the tooth can be extracted.

The function of the pulp was described in Chapter 2. It was noted that when the pulp is removed the tooth is 'dead'. For a root canal filled tooth, damage to the dentine should not cause pain. Also the pulp can no longer fulfil the role of replacing dentine. This lack of renewal means that the tooth can deteriorate over time and root canal filled teeth are always more brittle than 'live' teeth. A tooth that has been root-filled and then received a filling on the crown will very likely eventually need an artificial crown. The roots themselves may become non-viable after a period of years so that extraction becomes the only alternative left.

In terms of choice, for front teeth it is almost certainly preferable to have root canal treatment and a crown if necessary. Even for back teeth there are strong arguments for keeping roots in place if possible. These arguments will be discussed in detail in Chapter 11 which deals with extractions. Case Study 9 in Chapter 5 is an example of a patient exercising choice in this area. Readers should certainly use the detail given in this book in order to discuss the possibilities with their dentist. As stated earlier, endodontics is an area of dentistry where changes are happening all the time. There is certainly much more emphasis now on saving any part of a tooth if possible. Virtually all dentists are interested in keeping up with change and will be very pleased if patients show an educated interest in possibilities for treatment.

The use of artificial crowns

Artificial crowns are made individually to match the original crown. They are made in a in a dental laboratory. The dentist has to make an impression of the tooth requirement which is then sent off to the laboratory for processing. This means that any fitting of an artificial crown will need at least two visits to the dentist. These artificial crowns are generally made of a metal and porcelain. The metal can be either gold or nickel alloy. Such crowns are known either as porcelain bonded crowns (PBC) or porcelain jacket crowns (PJC). The porcelain can be matched precisely in colour and the metal gives the strength. For a front tooth the metal can be seen at the back of the crown by using a mirror placed in the mouth to reflect on to a bathroom or similar vertical mirror. For a back tooth the metal is bonded underneath the porcelain. Temporary crowns are fitted while the permanent crowns are being manufactured. A small version of a crown, which is often fitted for cosmetic purposes, is known as a veneer. Veneers are generally made of porcelain only. The use of a veneer attached by an adhesive can be an alternative to a filling of composite resin or glass ionomer cement attached using the acid etching technique as discussed in Chapter 9.

The procedure for fitting crowns starts with the preparation for keeping the crown in place. This involves either shaping dentine or fitting a post, as in figures 10.1 or 10.3. The process of shaping the dentine can be fairly involved.

For good adhesion of the crown, the sides of the protrusion and shoulders (officially known as the protozoon) as in Figure 10.1 need to be as near vertical as possible. Sometimes, in order to provide a good shape and size for the protozoon, it will have to be enlarged by adding filling material. This material may also have to be strengthened with tiny pins screwed into the dentine (rather like reinforced concrete).

The dentist will then take an impression of the area where the tooth is located. In order to make the impression the patient has to bite into a soft rubbery-like material which then hardens after a minute or so and can be taken from the mouth. Very often an impression will also be taken of the opposing teeth in order that the technician making the crown can check the occlusion. A temporary crown is then fitted using weak cement. It usually takes around ten days or two weeks for the permanent crown to be made. On a subsequent visit the permanent crown is checked for a good fit and good occlusion and if these are satisfactory the crown is cemented into place. Artificial crowns can last for many years. Somewhere between 5 and 30 years is normal. Crowns can become loose or displaced, especially fairly soon after fitting. If the patient takes the crown back to the dentist, they can usually be easily re-cemented on to their anchor point. It is sensible to have crowned teeth examined by a dentist once a year or so. This examination will usually include an X-ray.

Table of costs

The basis for the figures are given in Chapter 9. The figures in the table are for 1996 and are approximate to the nearest £. Where there are two figures, the top figure in each space is the minimum level of charge and the bottom figure is the maximum. The minimum figure is for routine work and is therefore the most likely figure that will occur.

Treatment	NHS	I	II	III	IV
Root canal treatment	18 42	45 80	60 100	70 120	80 140
Fitting a post	9 18	20 44	25 60	29 68	35 76
Fitting a crown PBC/PJC	39 60	109 156	145 203	170 238	193 271
Fitting a crown Gold	65 70	140 150	175 187	200 214	300 320
Composite back filling	N/A	15 45	19 57	25 75	34 102
Veneer	50	134	180	209	238

Chapter 11

Extractions

replacement of lost teeth with bridges or dentures

Summary level

This chapter discusses the options and procedures that follow from a decision that one or more teeth have to be extracted. As many readers will know, the loss of teeth, and in particular the first loss of a permanent tooth, is quite a traumatic experience. The person concerned needs to realise this fact, and their family can help them by providing sympathy and support. One of the main purposes of this chapter is to give readers an understanding of the nature of the choice between bridges and dentures when extractions have left gaps in natural teeth. Another major purpose is to provide help for people who are wearing partial or full dentures, or who are about to have dentures fitted. The summary level in this chapter is considerably longer that for any other chapter because there is a lot of low level information that can be helpful for everybody who is having teeth extracted.

Once it has been decided that teeth are to be extracted, then the dentist and patient need to discuss options for temporary and permanent replacements. If the extraction affects appearance, especially for front teeth, then many patients are likely to want an immediate temporary replacement. There can be other unpleasant consequences if gaps are left where teeth have been lost. Opposing and adjacent teeth soon start to cause problems by growing or moving to fill the space. Caries and Gingivitis (see Chapter 6) in these teeth can then develop very quickly. Speech and efficiency of mastication can also be affected. Gaps must be filled quickly and this chapter is largely concerned with the various ways in which artificial teeth can be placed in positions previously occupied by lost natural teeth. The branch of dentistry concerned with this replacement of lost teeth by artificial teeth is known as 'Prosthetics' or 'Prosthodontics'.

Another factor that needs to be considered in relation to extraction is that the supporting bone structures of the teeth change after teeth are extracted. This bone structure, known as the 'alveolar process', has a natural ridge just below the gum margin of the teeth (see Figure 6.2). When the tooth is extracted then the ridge shrinks and contracts. For a single tooth these changes are not significant, but if a row of adjacent teeth, or all the teeth, are extracted then the shrinking process can change the shape and form of the mouth (see Case Study 8 in Chapter 5).

The detailed level for this chapter starts by describing the way that extractions are carried out and the precautions that have to be taken during and after extraction. Control of bleeding and guarding against infection are the main aspects that need care and attention by the patient.

The main problem with artificial replacements for lost natural teeth is keeping them rigidly in place. If a person has lost all their natural teeth, then they are described technically as 'edentulous'. Someone who is edentulous will need a set of full dentures which have to be kept in place by 'suction'. This means that the dentures have to be a perfect fit to the mouth and gums so that there is a very fine, fully continuous, moisture film between the denture and the surfaces of the mouth. If this moisture film is disturbed and air enters, then the denture will become loose. The methods for achieving this result and dealing with possible problems are discussed in detail in this chapter. If natural teeth or roots are present then the artificial replacements for lost teeth can be kept rigidly in place by being connected in some way to these natural teeth or roots. There are many different ways of achieving these rigid replacements. Factors affecting the way of achieving rigidity are the number of teeth needing replacing and the number of natural teeth or roots left. The most common of these methods of replacement are discussed in this chapter under the headings of bridges, full dentures, partial dentures and overdentures.

In many cases readers are likely to be offered a straight choice between a bridge or a denture to fill gaps. The advantage of bridges is that they are permanently fixed and so seem more natural. On the other hand bridges can be considerably more expensive than dentures. Bridges are mostly used to fill a gap when a single tooth has been extracted, though more complex bridges can be used for multiple extractions. Bridges are individually designed to be rigidly attached to remaining teeth and to contain artificial teeth to fill spaces caused by extractions. The teeth used for attachment to the bridge need to be modified to receive the bridge. The details of the construction and fitting of two types of bridge are given in this chapter.

Full dentures are fitted when a patient has lost all their teeth. Bridges, partial dentures and overdentures are used when some complete teeth or roots of teeth remain. A major difference between dentures and bridges is that the denture can be removed by the wearer but the bridge cannot.

In this chapter, details concerning full dentures are discussed before partial dentures and overdentures. There are two reasons for this choice of order. Firstly it will enable readers to realise the implications of receiving full dentures before reading about alternatives. Secondly many of the procedures for fitting partial dentures and overdentures are similar to full dentures. The procedures for fitting full dentures are described by breaking the process down into five stages. These stages relate to the minimum number of five visits to the dentist needed to extract teeth and fit full dentures. Changing to full dentures is a big step for anybody and people undergoing this stage need all the help possible. If they and friends and relatives read this chapter carefully it will be of considerable help. Partial dentures can be used if some teeth remain and can be used for their natural function and as a support for the denture. Overdentures can be used if parts of some teeth remain and a denture can be made that will fit over the remnants. In this case the natural teeth are covered by artificial teeth. The fitting of partial dentures and overdentures is described by comparing the process to the fitting of full dentures.

A common problem with both full and partial dentures is that the surface of the mouth under the plate supporting the denture becomes sore. This soreness is normally caused by an infection, and can usually be cured by not wearing the denture unless it is absolutely necessary and using a mouth wash that can be bought from chemists for this purpose. If problems persist then the person should see a dentist. Too high a sugar intake and other dietary factors can help to cause this problem.

It is also possible to use a metal or plastic implant to replace a missing root, but this treatment is rare and is discussed in Chapter 15. It is also possible to use implants as anchors for overdentures which then become an alternative to full dentures. Case Study 11 in Chapter 5 is an illustration of the use of this procedure. Case Studies 8, 10, and 12 in Chapter 5, and Questions 3 and 4 in Chapter 4 are also relevant to this chapter.

At the end of the detailed level in this chapter there is a table with estimates of costs for the different treatments covered in the chapter.

Detailed level

Extractions

Extraction has a long history as a dental treatment. Teeth have been extracted as a remedy for dental problems going back at least 5000 years. Nobody likes the idea of having teeth extracted and it is worth noting the reasons why extraction has to be used. Two common diseases that can involve extraction as a treatment are caries and periodontal disease as discussed in Chapter 6. For these diseases, extraction should usually be suggested as a last resort and should only be used either if there are reasons why restorative treatment is not going to be effective, or all possible restorative treatments have been tried and have failed. Extraction may also be the only option after severe accidental damage to a tooth. It may also occasionally happen that a patient who has already lost many teeth needs a partial denture. In this case natural teeth left may sometimes conflict with the most sensible design for the denture. Such teeth may then be extracted. It is also possible that a tooth may be extracted for cosmetic reasons or as a part of orthodontic treatment if there is not enough space on a patient's jaw.

The actual mechanics of basic extraction are simple. Teeth are extracted using forceps. These forceps are inserted between the gum and the tooth until it is possible to achieve a firm grip well down the root of the tooth. There are many different types of forceps. Which type is used depends on the position of the tooth and the preferences of the dentist. The dentist has to push the forceps quite hard to go well down the root and this pressure may be felt by the patient. The tooth is then eased out with a gentle rocking movement rather than a straight pull. Given an effective local anaesthetic the patient should feel no pain. A surgical extraction is used if the roots are damaged or distorted, but in this case the condition will have been diagnosed before the extraction is attempted and the patient will have been informed that the procedure will differ from normal.

The main immediate problem with extraction is bleeding. It is important that a blood clot should form in the socket as soon as possible. Care has to be taken to ensure that this clot is not then subsequently disturbed. After an extraction, a patient may be asked to bite on a pad over the socket in order to apply pressure and facilitate the formation of a blood clot in the socket. The patient should not be allowed to leave the surgery until the bleeding has stopped. For the next twenty-four hours the patient then has to take great care not to disturb the clot. Keeping food and hot liquids well away from the site and avoiding strenuous exercise and alcohol are strongly recommended. If bleeding does start again then a judgement has to be made of how serious it is. A small amount of blood mixed with saliva is natural and can be ignored. If it looks as though the clot has gone then using a pressure pad of sterile gauze, similar to that given after the extraction, may help. Heavy subsequent bleeding may need urgent help from the dentist or a doctor. Such treatment known as 'arrest of haemorrhage' is free under NHS provision.

A complication of extraction which can arise after a few days is known as a 'dry socket' or a 'septic socket'. This condition is extremely painful and is caused by the bone in the socket becoming infected. A dry socket will need urgent treatment by a dentist. If a blood clot forms immediately after extraction and is not disturbed then a dry socket is very unlikely to happen. Another main consequence of extraction is that the patient is likely to feel significant pain for up to 48 hours after the extraction. This pain can be eased with standard pain-killing drugs. As aspirin can encourage bleeding it may be sensible to avoid this drug after extractions.

People who have a tooth extracted for the first time will often find the experience traumatic. It is after all losing a part of your body. Not quite as bad as losing a finger, but still a very unpleasant experience. Support from families and friends is important. If the tooth involved is a front tooth then it is likely to be replaced by an 'immediate denture'. This denture has to be designed and made before the extraction and is then fitted immediately after the extraction. Such dentures will often only last for a short period of time (usually around 2/6 months) because of the changes in the bone structure after extraction.

Bridges

Bridges are designed to enable artificial teeth to be permanently attached to natural teeth. There is a major distinction between dentures and bridges. Dentures can be removed by the patient but bridges cannot be removed. Bridges therefore stay in place all the time and seem much more natural for the patient. They are cleaned as a part of the normal teeth cleaning process, and eating processes like biting and chewing do not have to be modified because of the presence of a bridge. There are various ways of attaching bridges to natural teeth. Three diagrams will be used to illustrate the general methods, procedures and problems associated with the use of bridges.

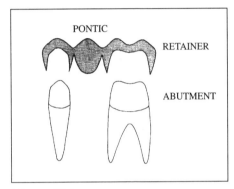

Figure 11.1

Figure 11.1 illustrates the most common way of using a bridge to establish a permanent artificial replacement for a natural tooth. The two adjacent teeth have to be prepared to receive crowns as described in Chapter 10. When crowns are fitted to teeth in order to fit a bridge, the teeth involved are known as 'abutments'. There are two abutments shown in Figure 11.1, only one of which is labelled. A section of the bridge which forms a crown that fits onto an abutment is known as a 'retainer'. There are two retainers in this case. In the construction of a bridge, the replacement for the missing tooth or teeth is known as the 'pontic'. Bridges can have many different designs. Some bridges have only one abutment, but such bridges are usually used for incisors and the abutment is not necessarily an adjacent tooth. Bridges of that kind have a curved connection which lays on the surface of the mouth. Bridges for back teeth sometimes have pontics which leave a considerable space between the pontic and the gum. The space facilitates cleaning.

It can be seen that the construction of effective bridges is similar to building road bridges in that it involves complex engineering principles in order to achieve rigidity, safety and lasting wear under a variety of external conditions. The appearance of bridges can be very natural. Like artificial crowns bridges can be made of metal with porcelain bonding. The sections connecting the pontic to the abutments are constructed so that they hardly show. Much more complex bridges which provide replacements for more than one missing tooth can be used. The decision whether to use a bridge or a partial denture or a mixture of these can involve many factors. These include the age and occupation of the patient, as well as the state of teeth to be used as possible abutments. The prognosis for other teeth also needs consideration, as it would not make sense to install an expensive bridge if other nearby teeth are likely to need to be extracted in two or three years time. The details given in this book should help readers to be more involved in this decision making process.

When bridges like the one illustrated in Figure 11.1 are used the abutments have to receive artificial crowns. As discussed in Chapter 10, the fitting of such crowns means that the teeth involved have to have their natural crowns removed. If these natural crowns are in good condition then removing them might seem a heavy price to pay in order to fill the gap caused by the missing tooth. One way of avoiding the loss of the crowns on abutments is illustrated in Figures 11.2. and 11.3.

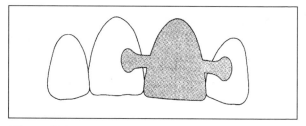

Figure 11.2

Figure 11.2 shows the back view of a bridge for a front tooth. The shaded section is the metal backing for the pontic. It has two wing like attachments which are attached to the abutments by composite fillings and acid etching as described in Chapter 9 on fillings.

Figure 11.3

Figure 11.3 is a side view of an abutment tooth for this type of bridge and shows that the abutment tooth is very little affected by the bridge. These bridges are known as 'Maryland' bridges. They are much easier to make than conventional bridges. Maryland bridges are most commonly used for front teeth on younger patients.

The procedure for fitting bridges is very similar to crowns. The bridges have to be made in a dental laboratory, so that receiving a bridge will involve at least two visits. On the first visit the abutments have to be prepared and impressions taken. These impressions are then sent to the dental laboratory, where making the bridge is likely to take up to two weeks. In the interval, temporary crowns will be fitted to the abutments. A gap caused by a missing front tooth can be filled with an immediate denture as described earlier in this chapter. Some relatively straightforward bridges can have a temporary version made up at the dentist's chair. When the permanent bridge is ready to be fitted, the occlusion will be carefully checked. Minor modifications can be carried out by the dentist if necessary. The bridge is then fixed using strong cement or by acid etching if it is a Maryland bridge.

Standard bridges as represented by Figure 11.1 can be expected to last between five and twenty years. Problems with caries or periodontal disease in the abutments are a common cause of failure, so personal care and regular dental check-ups are essential. The loss of the natural crowns on abutments discourage some readers from undergoing this treatment. However, it is very often the case that the potential abutments already have fillings. In this case the crown fitted as the retainer for the pontic can act as a guard against further caries attack on the abutment. The only other slight drawback is the extra wear on the root of the abutment which might be caused by the abutment having to withstand the forces exerted on the pontic. The condition of the potential abutments is a very important factor when considering the use of a bridge as a treatment. Maryland bridges can have problems with the flanges adhering to the abutments. The abutments have to be completely sound, so that acid etching can be applied to a thick layer of enamel. The preparation of the abutments and the attaching process has to be done very carefully in totally dry conditions.

Full dentures

The number of people in the UK who are edentulous and so need full dentures has decreased significantly over the last twenty years, from over 30% to under 20% of the total adult population. This decreasing trend is certain to continue because of the increased emphasis on keeping natural teeth and the more sophisticated treatments available to assist in their retention. Only a small percentage of elderly people are likely to become edentulous in the next millennium. Meanwhile there are still many people who have full dentures and many more who will need them eventually. Readers may have elderly relatives with full dentures so the details in this section should help them to realise how they might help these relatives. There will be other readers who are at the stage of losing several teeth and this section will then provide the information needed for decision making. The most likely route for progression to full dentures is by way of bridges, partial dentures and possibly overdentures. This is in contrast to removing all remaining teeth at once and having to acquire the skill of using full dentures without any intervening stages. The details in this section and the next two sections on partial dentures and overdentures need to be read in this context of progression.

As stated at the beginning of this chapter, full dentures are largely kept in place by 'suction'. One way of illustrating the way this 'suction' works is to wet a small piece of newspaper about the size of the roof of the mouth and to attach it to the bottom of a horizontal surface like an overhead kitchen cabinet. The newspaper will stick to the surface because atmospheric pressure is holding it there, with the water giving a seal between the paper and the surface of the cabinet. If the piece of paper is left to dry it will fall because the seal becomes ineffective. Unlike the piece of newspaper, the seal for denture stays in place because the moisture, in the form of saliva, is constantly replaced. This principle keeps the denture in place in the vertical plane, or for up-and-down motion, and is known as providing 'mucosal support'. The situation for the horizontal plane, or backward and forward motion, is different. The denture is made to be a close fit to the ridge that remains from where the teeth protruded. This ridge will then inhibit movement of the denture in and out of the mouth to some extent. The wearers of full denture also have to work at keeping them in place by use of muscular actions with the jaws and tongue. A graphic way of describing the skills of using full dentures is that the wearer has to practise 'oral gymnastics'. The wearers of full dentures also have to be careful in choosing what to eat and how to eat it. For example they should avoid very sticky toffee and employ a different technique for biting apples. After a while such actions become natural. If dentures are well fitted and the user is fully acclimatised then they will often say that wearing dentures seems natural and using them causes no problems.

This discussion about the use of full dentures may seem somewhat protracted, but it is necessary in order to understand the complexity of the procedure for making and fitting full dentures. Before moving on to procedures there are two other general points to be made. The first is that, because the use of full dentures is not straightforward and depends on accuracy of fit and the patient learning new techniques for eating and speaking, then people do need to have both dentures and technique updated on a regular once-a-year basis. The second point is that full dentures can never be as efficient as natural teeth. A general estimate is that they are at best 30% as efficient as a full set of natural teeth.

As with bridges, dentures are made in a dental laboratory. Full dentures are made of pink acrylic with natural-looking artificial teeth attached. It is possible to mount the acrylic on a metal plate for increased strength. We have already seen that full dentures have to be a very good fit to the surface of the mouth. The teeth must also be fitted so that biting and other muscle action does not cause displacement and the dentures must not interfere with speech. Considering that all these conditions have to be satisfied in a three-dimensional moving space, it can be seen that achieving a good result is not easy.

The fitting of a set of full dentures will require at least four visits to the dentist. The procedures for starting with some natural teeth and receiving a set of full dentures are divided into five stages.

Fitting full dentures – stage 1

The first stage is to remove any remaining teeth and check that there are no retained roots and that the surfaces in the mouth that will support the denture are healthy. From the point of view of the patient, it is likely that this stage will be related to an extension of experiences with partial dentures and problems with remaining natural teeth. Stage 1 may also be integrated with stage 2 in terms of the actual visit to the dentist.

Fitting full dentures – stage 2

Stage 2 involves the generation of suitable base plates on which the teeth will be fitted. During the visit impressions will be taken of the gums and surfaces of the mouth. These impressions are taken by inserting an impression tray carrying a paste which sets like jelly over the gums and palate. Some people find this sensation unpleasant. At this stage the dentist will also note what the extent of the base plates should be in order to provide a maximum contact with saliva-bearing surfaces, without interfering with speech or tongue movement. From this point of view, the supporting plates for upper teeth can be more extensive than plates for lower teeth. This is because the roots of the tongue take up space on the lower palate. Figure 11.4. illustrates this difference. One consequence of the greater surface contact for the supporting plates of an upper set of full dentures is that upper teeth often feel more secure to the patient when they first receive dentures.

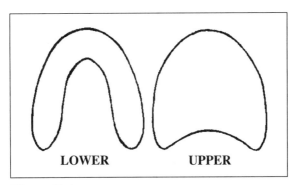

LOWER   **UPPER**

Figure 11.4

The impressions for the upper and lower jaw and the appropriate measurements are then sent to the dental laboratory. A technician will use the impressions and measurements in order to make temporary base plates with a wax rim positioned on the plates in the approximate position where the teeth will be fitted. These temporary base plates are known as 'occlusion rims'.

Fitting full dentures – stage 3

The purpose of this stage is to make sure the teeth will be correctly positioned and angled and that the dentures will work efficiently in their three dimensional space. In order to understand what problems there may be, consider people you know who have a bottom jaw that juts out, while others have a jaw that recedes. It is possible that the gum impressions for both of these people might look very similar, but the way the teeth are fitted and the dentures allowed to move in the vertical plane will have to be very different. For the patient this stage will involve fitting the occlusion rims and then trying them for correctness and comfort. The dentist will then take measurements which record the relationship of the jaws at rest. This process is known as taking the 'occlusal registration' or more commonly as 'taking the bite'. It is also at this stage that the colour and nature of the teeth should be discussed. One bonus of full dentures is that the patient can make cosmetic decisions about their future teeth rather than having to accept what they were given in the way of natural teeth. A common mistake made by people starting to wear full dentures is to choose teeth that are too white. Pure white teeth look very unnatural.

Fitting full dentures – stage 4

In this stage a set of trial full dentures is made and tested. The occlusal rims and other measurements and details generated in stage 3 are sent to the laboratory. The technician uses a device known as an 'articulator' to help with the next part of the manufacturing process. An articulator is a hinged mechanism, designed to model the movement of jaws, which can be adjusted to suit measurements of individual patients sent by dentists. The occlusal rims are fitted to the articulator and suitable teeth fixed temporarily with wax. Adjustments can then be made by simulating actions of the mouth. On the next visit to the dental surgery, these trial dentures are then fitted by the dentist into the patients mouth in order to see if they fit correctly, generate a good occlusion and are acceptable in appearance and feel to the patient. This process is known as the 'try in' and is a very important occasion for the patient. While the patient cannot expect the trial full dentures to look perfect or feel fully comfortable, they must voice any misgivings at this stage. It is probably a good idea to take a close relative or friend for this visit in order to give support and reassurance. If necessary an extra appointment to try dentures can be made, after the dentures have been modified in the laboratory; the procedure is then sometimes called a 're-try'.

Fitting full dentures – stage 5

Stage 5 involves the making and fitting of the final set of full dentures. The trial dentures are returned to the laboratory, together with notes on any adjustments that need to be made. The technician will then make the final version. At the patient's next visit, the dentist will show the patient how to fit the final full denture. The occlusion and closeness of fit will be checked and some minor adjustments can be made by the dentist if necessary. Advice on immediate use and ways of adapting to the dentures will also be given: the teeth should be left in place day and night for two or three days in order for the mouth to become acclimatised; after that the dentures should be removed each night and kept in water because if acrylic dries it can become misshapen; the dentures should be cleaned after meals in cool water, using proper dental products; cleaning should be done with the dentures held over a bowl of water or a towel in case the dentures are dropped. Acrylic can break easily if it falls on to a hard surface; it is also best to hold dentures in the middle, rather than the ends, as a grip on the end might lead to a force exerted on the middle, which could cause a fracture. The patient will also be given an appointment for around two weeks later so that progress can be monitored.

With modern materials and techniques, plus the use of care in the production process, full dentures should allow people to keep a good appearance and to be able to eat efficiently. Unlike other treatments for natural teeth, it is not possible to say that full dentures will last for a longish period of time like, for example, five to ten years. The reason for this lack of predictability is that when all natural teeth have been extracted, a process known as 'resorption' occurs. Resorption means that the bone structure that supported the teeth gradually becomes absorbed into the jaw bone. The result of this process is that the section of the mouth that was the gum margin gradually reduces in size. This process will continue through the patient's like but has more immediate results in the early stages. Full dentures will therefore need adjustment and replacement on a more or less continuous basis. Annual visits to a dentist are an absolute priority if appearance and health are to be maintained. If full dentures are not adjusted then resorption can over time completely change the shape of the lower face. The nose can almost meet the chin! As well as efficiency of mastication, speech can also be affected. Readers with elderly relatives may need to emphasise these facts and try to ensure an annual visit, maybe by making the visit a part of birthday celebrations and going along to provide support. Case Study 12 in Chapter 5 illustrates problems that occur if somebody with full dentures does not have regular check-ups.

The details given in this section reinforce the need for new users of full dentures to realise that their use requires adjustments in day-to-day processes. Eating and perhaps speaking methods need to change, the muscles of the mouth, tongue and lips have to learn new responses. Patience will be required in order to adjust. Learning to use dentures in this way is at least as difficult as learning to drive a car.

Partial dentures

The term partial dentures is used to describe dentures that replace some, but not all, natural teeth. Partial dentures therefore perform a similar function to bridges. Unlike bridges, partial dentures are not permanently fixed. Partial dentures can be removed by the wearer. Bridges are most commonly used where there are gaps from the removal of no more than two adjacent teeth. If there are more than two adjacent teeth missing then a partial denture is more likely to be suggested as the best solution. As can be imagined, an upper or lower set of sixteen teeth can have all sorts of combinations of missing teeth, so the design of partial dentures can be very complex. One major difference to full dentures is that the presence of some natural teeth enables the partial denture to be secured to remaining teeth. The partial denture then has mechanical support in contrast to a full denture which has to rely solely on mucosal support. Mechanical support makes the denture much more secure. The artificial teeth on a partial denture will also have to match remaining natural teeth in colour, size, position and orientation, so cutting down on some aspects of decision making and complexity of manufacture in comparison with full dentures.

Partial dentures are usually retained in position by clasps that fasten on to remaining natural teeth. Natural teeth can also be used to provide vertical support for the denture or to keep it fixed in the horizontal plane. Natural teeth that are going to be used for clasps or to provide support or to stop movement often have to be modified by adding filling material, providing a groove for tiny metal rods to engage, or receiving a fine in-built metal strip onto which the denture will locate. Such fittings are known as 'precision attachments'. Partial dentures can also have mucosal support like full dentures, or they can be designed to have a mixture of mechanical and mucosal support.

There are two alternative construction materials for partial dentures. These alternatives are acrylic only or a metal structure with acrylic additions. Most partial dentures in the UK are made of acrylic only, apart from the clasps. The acrylic only alternative is cheaper and more flexible as acrylic dentures can easily be modified if there are changes in the wearer's dental circumstances. The big advantage of a metal base is that the dentures can provide more strength in a less bulky form. The denture is therefore likely to be more inconspicuous in terms of appearance. The metal and acrylic alternative for dentures is more expensive to make and fit. The use of metal based partial dentures is sensible for situations where they are expected to last a long time, longer than five years for example.

An additional feature for the design of partial dentures is the need for the wearer to be able to remove and replace them easily. A partial denture can have as many as three clasps and also have rods and grooves that need to engage exactly with fittings on natural teeth. The procedure for removing and replacing such a denture can be quite complex. The path for insertion may also not be vertical but come from the back of the mouth.

For the patient, the procedures and stages for fitting partial dentures are almost the same as those already given for full dentures. The only major difference is that the try in at stage 4 may be done with what will be the final denture rather than a temporary set. From the patient's point of view this difference does not affect the nature of the experience.

Partial dentures vary considerably in the length of time they can be expected to last and in the way that background factors like resorption and disease might affect their efficiency and functioning lifetime. Wear on remaining natural teeth can be caused by the clasps and other fittings on the denture. Consistent and careful oral hygiene is essential for wearers of partial dentures. Dentists can be wary of suggesting partial dentures for patients if they think that the patient in question will not be able to maintain the necessary level of oral hygiene. Both the denture and the natural teeth need to be cleaned at least once a day and with some dentures, after every meal. Regular check-up visits to the dentist are also essential.

A partial denture can be used as a first temporary replacement when a front tooth is extracted. This will sometimes be the first time that the person concerned has a 'foreign body' resident in their mouth and it can be difficult adjusting to this new situation. They might find that excess saliva is produced and that the denture tends to move slightly under pressure. It usually takes about a week for the denture to feel reasonably natural and this temporary denture should be replaced with either a more permanent version or a bridge after a period of about six months.

Overdentures

Overdentures are made to fit over retained roots and reduced crowns of natural teeth. The patient is therefore not edentulous. Overdentures can be used as an alternative to, or combined with, either full dentures or partial dentures. The very big advantage of this situation is that the presence of roots of natural teeth means that there is no resorption of the supporting bone of the teeth. The gum margin stays in its original position and the shape of the face is not subject to change.

Overdentures can be kept in place by mucosal support, in the same way as full dentures. It is also possible to supply other means of support by using the remaining natural teeth. As the natural remnants of teeth are underneath the denture, it is not possible to use clasps as with partial dentures. The support has to be activated by just pushing the denture in place. An analogy might be with clothing and the use of press studs or velcro to keep two sections together. Similar devices can be fitted to the denture and natural teeth in order to help with adhesion. As can be imagined such devices need precision engineering and so are expensive in terms of both time and money. An overdenture fixed in this way is called an 'overdenture with precision attachments'.

For the patient the procedure and stages for fitting overdentures will be very similar to those listed for full dentures. The use of overdentures in the UK is rare. Besides being difficult and time-consuming to make, they can also need frequent and painstaking maintenance. It is possible that some dentists may not suggest overdentures as an alternative when the particular situation of impending loss of more natural teeth arises. The big plus of receiving overdentures rather than full dentures is the possibility of postponing the edentulous state for many more years. On the other hand the use of overdentures will need meticulous oral hygiene by the wearer and possible expensive maintenance and repair by the dentist. The details given here should help readers who are near this stage, or who have relatives who are near this stage, to consider the use of overdentures and be fully involved in the decision making process. Case Study 11 in Chapter 5 illustrates the use of implants and an overdenture as an alternative to a full denture.

Table of costs

The costs of the treatments covered in this chapter are very varied. Having read the chapter, readers will realise that there can be very complex solutions to particular situations of missing teeth, with corresponding increases in costs. Gold can be used as the metal base which can also increase costs further. The figures for private practice should therefore be seen even more as a rough guide than the figures in the previous two chapters.

The figure for **extraction** is for a single tooth. If more than one tooth is extracted the figure will increase, though not necessarily on a per tooth basis.

Bridges can be very expensive, especially if they are to replace more than one tooth. The maximum figure given in the table could well be exceeded.

The figures for **partial dentures** are for a single denture, i.e. for either the upper or lower jaw. The figures for full dentures are for both jaws.

It is possible to have a **full denture** for one jaw only and the cost of this will be rather more than half the figure given under full dentures.

The cost of **immediate dentures** are very similar to permanent dentures.

The figures for **overdentures** are for overdentures with precision attachments.

The cost of overdentures that do not have precision attachments will be roughly the same as the cost of full dentures.

The basis for the figures are given at the end of Chapter 9. The figures in the table are for 1996 and are approximate to the nearest £. Where there are two figures, the top figure in each space is the minimum level of charge and the bottom figure is the maximum. The minimum figure is for routine work and is therefore the most likely figure that will occur.

Treatment	NHS	I	II	III	IV
Extraction	9	15	20	25	30
Bridges	160 300	200 800	250 1000	300 1200	350 1400
Maryland Bridge	100	200	250	50	400
Partial denture Acrylic only	33 59	120 184	150 244	175 305	200 366
Partial denture Metal and Acrylic	84 94	267 302	356 404	445 510	534 650
Full denture Acrylic	80	250	275	375	500
Full denture metal and Acrylic	119	430	50	640	750
Overdenture	160	550	600	650	700
Temporary bridge	15	22	26	32	40

Chapter 12

Periodontal treatment

for problems with gums

Summary level

The previous three chapters can be viewed as forming a progression in the treatment of tooth decay or caries. From fillings to root canal therapy, then to extraction, then to replacement of missing teeth. From that point of view, this chapter is a change in direction, because periodontal disease is concerned with the gums and the other supporting structures of teeth, rather than the teeth themselves. As an illustration of this difference, it is possible for a tooth to be extracted because of advanced periodontal disease, even though the tooth itself is in perfect condition.

As noted earlier (in Chapter 2), it is estimated that at any moment in time, over 80% of adults in the UK have periodontal disease at some level. One explanation for this is that periodontal disease is progressive over many years. During the first year or two, people can have periodontal disease at a low level and not even realise it. By the time symptoms like bleeding and pain appear, the disease is likely to have progressed to a relatively serious state. This late occurrence of recognisable symptoms is in almost complete contrast to caries, where pain with hot and cold substances occurs fairly early on in the progress of the disease.

Another aspect of periodontal disease, that has also been mentioned earlier, is that it is often caused by neglect. As an illustration of this fact, it is almost certain that the many people who now live rough on the streets, and who have not had the opportunity to clean their teeth for many years, will have advanced periodontal disease. By contrast, it is likely that anybody reading this book will have been practising careful oral hygiene for most of their lives, and will therefore be most unlikely to have periodontal disease at an advanced state. From the high figure of over 80% of adults with periodontal disease it is evident, however, that good oral hygiene is not sufficient on its own to ensure that the disease is not present.

The content of this chapter will help readers to understand the fundamental nature of the disease and to appreciate why it is so common. The place and limitations of oral hygiene in preventing the disease will become evident. While regular visits to a dentist are important for control of caries, they are fundamental in the control of periodontal disease. The reasons for this necessity of regular dental treatment will also be made clear by the details given in this chapter.

The detailed level starts with a description of the basic nature and causes of periodontal disease. There are also other relatively rare types of periodontal disease and a description of these follows next in the detailed level. The normal progression of periodontal disease has four reasonably well-defined stages which are described in depth at the detailed level and described in outline next at this level. Readers will find that reference to Figures 12.2, 12.3 and 12.5 will help them to follow this description. If the first stage is taken to be a normal healthy tooth and gum (Figure 12.2) then the second stage is a build-up of plaque and tartar between the tooth and the gum (Figure 12.2). Nearly every adult is at this stage most of the time, and the build-up is usually in a position where normal cleaning is ineffective. During regular visits to the dentist any occurrence of the disease at this level is easily treated with scaling and polishing in the affected area.

The third stage is reached when the build-up of tartar and resultant bacteria causes the gum to become detached from the tooth so forming a space known as a pocket (Figure 12.3). At this stage the gums start to become red, swollen and painful. Infected gums will also bleed when under pressure from a toothbrush or eating. At this third stage removal of the tartar may solve the problem but sometimes the gum does not return to its proper place in contact with the tooth. Treatment may then involve stitching the gum back into place or removing a part of the gum.

At the final stage (Figure 12.5) other supporting structures besides the gum are affected. These structures can be both the supporting bone and the ligament between the tooth and bone. The tooth itself can also become damaged. Minor oral surgery which consists of removing all diseased tissues and repositioning the gums can sometimes be a successful treatment of this stage but often extraction is the only sensible option. Periodontal disease can be a special problem when other factors are involved which encourage a rapid progression between stages. These factors are most likely to develop in teenagers and sometimes in people in-between twenty and forty years old.

The chapter concludes with a table giving estimates of costs for the treatments described in the chapter. Case Study 7 in Chapter 5 illustrates very clearly how a lack of personal dental care can soon cause serious gum disease problems.

Detailed level

Periodontal disease attacks the supporting structures of the teeth. Figure 12.1 shows the nature of these structures, known as the 'periodontum'.

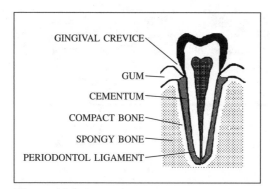

Figure 12.1

From Figure 12.1 it can be seen that the periodontum consists of the gums (or gingiva), the periodontal ligament, the compact bone and the spongy bone. It is when these sections of tissue are affected that periodontal disease is present. As the disease progresses from gums, to periodontal ligament, to compact bone, to spongy bone, it becomes progressively more serious.

The basic cause of periodontal disease is the action of a range of bacteria on supporting tissues of teeth. Human bodies, including the mouth, contain huge numbers of bacteria. It has been estimated that one hour after teeth have been cleaned there are more than one million bacteria on each square millimetre of every tooth. Most of these bacteria are harmless and many are necessary for the body to function successfully, but under certain conditions some of these bacteria will attack and destroy tissue. As an example, a low level of oxygen, which can be found if bacteria find their way underneath the gum, favours the development of a group of bacteria known as 'obligate anaerobes'. This group of bacteria are associated with the progression of periodontal disease.

Knowing that it is the action of bacteria that causes the disease also leads to an understanding of other ways that periodontal disease can develop. Some bacteria can build up in numbers or become unbalanced in relation to the body's defences because of other external factors such as pregnancy, illness and its treatment with drugs, diet and even stress. These and other external factors can cause the rapid onset and progression of periodontal disease even when good oral hygiene is being practised. This development of the disease from commonly occurring external causes is another reason why readers need to be aware of the early symptoms of periodontal disease.

The role of plaque and tartar in the development of periodontal disease follows on from the fact that the presence of certain bacteria in particular places is the cause of the disease. Plaque is the sticky semi-transparent, yellow/white substance that quickly forms on teeth and between teeth and gums. Plaque provides another home for bacteria and enables different forms of bacteria to develop. Efficient cleaning of teeth and natural actions remove plaque, but if plaque is not removed there are two further consequences. Firstly the presence of the plaque in the gingival crevice enables bacteria to start to infiltrate below the gum, and secondly tartar, which is a hard stone-like substance, starts to form.

From this brief description of the causes of periodontal disease it can be seen already how it follows a developmental path. The stages of this path and associated symptoms and treatment will be described next.

Figure 12.2 illustrates the way that periodontal disease begins. This figure and two others that appear in this chapter have also been used in Chapter 6.

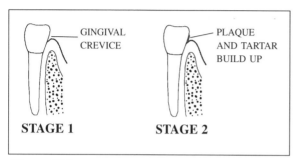

Figure 12.2

Stage 1 in this figure represents a normal tooth, free from periodontal disease. Stage 2 indicates the build-up of plaque and tartar (sometimes called 'calculus') in the gingival crevice. Stage 2 in Figure 12.2 represents the first stage of progression for the most common type of periodontal disease. Plaque forms naturally on teeth all the time. If this plaque is left undisturbed, then elements within the plaque react with saliva to generate tartar, which is a hard stone-like substance similar to the deposits left in kettles. Tartar cannot be removed by brushing. Given time this tartar can also become discoloured. Plaque forms on a daily basis, while tartar can form in a state visible by a dental professional within a period of two or three months. A heavy build-up of tartar with discolouration is likely to take one or two years. By the time this heavy build-up has happened, the presence of the tartar will have helped bacteria to infiltrate between the gum and the tooth and it is likely that the next stage of periodontal disease will also have been reached.

Efficient brushing removes plaque. Unfortunately people often have places where brushing is not totally effective, for example at the back of front teeth, at the front of back teeth, in-between teeth, where teeth are missing or crowded, where there are damaged fillings, or where there are orthodontic appliances or partial dentures. These places are also usually difficult for the person to see, so this stage of the progression of periodontal disease is not likely to be identified until the next visit to the dentist. At a regular routine visit, examination identifies tartar build-up, scaling removes any tartar and polishing removes any residual plaque. Every reader is likely to have received this scaling and polishing treatment. Such treatment needs to be a regular feature for the control of periodontal disease.

Figure 12.3 illustrates the next stage for the progression of the most common form of periodontal disease.

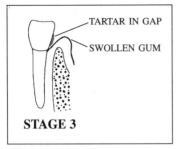

TARTAR IN GAP

SWOLLEN GUM

STAGE 3

Figure 12.3

The main distinction between stage 2 and stage 3 as shown in the diagrams is that the tartar has progressed to below the normal gum margin and the action of bacteria has loosened the gum from the tooth. In reality this change is likely to take place over a period of at least several months. The change will also be graduated in that plaque and bacteria will infiltrate under the gum before tartar starts to form. While the position indicated by Figure 12.2 might not qualify as periodontal disease, the position indicated by Figure 12.3 certainly does qualify. When the disease has reached the stage indicated by Figure 12.3 it is called 'chronic gingivitis'.

As a part of the progression to chronic gingivitis particular symptoms are likely. These indicate a serious problem and should be dealt with by a visit to the dentist. The first symptom is a change in the appearance of the gum margin, i.e. where the gum meets the tooth. The colour of the gum changes from pale pink to darker pink or red and the gum can be swollen. The second symptom is the presence of blood when cleaning the teeth. Some of the bacteria that flourish between a tooth and a gum attack the gum surface and make minute holes or ulcers. These ulcers bleed under pressure such as the application of a toothbrush. The presence of blood on a toothbrush, or mixed with saliva and toothpaste after cleaning teeth, is therefore a symptom of chronic gingivitis. Any such symptom should trigger a swift request for an appointment to see a dentist.

Chronic gingivitis as represented by Figure 12.3 can usually be treated by scaling and polishing. The scaling has to be very thorough, especially on the area of tooth that should have been below the gum. This scaling can be painful and might need an anaesthetic to be administered. The patient might have to use a mouth rinse for the following week in order to promote healing and to encourage infected gums to shrink. Advice on methods to avoid a recurrence of the disease in the affected area, by appropriate oral hygiene, is also likely to be given as in Case Study 7 in Chapter 5.

The gap between the tooth and the gum shown in Figure 12.3 is known to dental professionals as a 'pocket' or more exactly as a 'false pocket' in contrast to a 'true pocket' which appears at the next stage. The existence and depth of these pockets is a fundamental part of diagnosis for the presence and severity of periodontal disease. Before moving on to the next stage, it will be useful to look at an instrument that is used for measuring pocket depth.

Figure 12.4 is a diagrammatic representation of an instrument used for measuring pocket depths when periodontal disease is suspected. From the graduations of 3.5 and 5.5 mms shown on the diagram it can be seen that this is a very small instrument. The overall length is around 1.5 cms or about 3/4 of an inch.

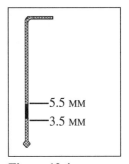

Figure 12.4

This particular instrument is the World Health Organisation's (WHO) periodontal probe. There are other commonly used instruments for measuring pocket depth. The WHO instrument is used as an illustration here for two reasons. Firstly the fact that the World Health Organisation has felt it necessary to produce such an instrument is another indication of the high incidence of periodontal disease and the importance of keeping the disease under control. Secondly the instrument is used specifically to help with a classification of the stage that periodontal disease has reached. This classification is defined in terms of the amount of the black section on the instrument that shows when the instrument is inserted into a pocket.

The classification is registered by giving a score as follows:-

Score 1 – All the black section between 3.5 and 5.5 mms shows
Score 2 – As Score 1, but tartar is present
Score 3 – Only a part of the black section shows
Score 4 – None of the black section shows

These scores correspond approximately to the four stages indicated in Figures 12.2, 12.3 and 12.5 in this chapter.

Figure 12.5 illustrates the final stage for the progression of the most common form of periodontal disease.

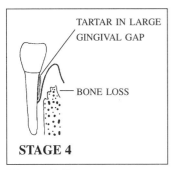

Figure 12.5

Referring back to Figure 12.1, it can be seen that the progression to Stage 4 involves a steady advance of the tartar and plaque plus associated bacteria along the root of the tooth. Figure 12.5 shows that a large part of the periodontal ligament and some bone has been destroyed by bacteria. Symptoms at this stage might include the tooth being loose, plus pain and severe infection of the tissues. The patient is also quite likely to have bad breath. The pocket is now called a 'true pocket', the black section on the WHO probe would not be visible and when the probe is inserted it is likely to generate an eruption of blood and pus at the bottom of the socket. The name given to the disease when it has reached this stage is 'chronic periodontitis'. The progression from stage 3 to stage 4 is a continuous process. The distinction between the two stages might be far from clear in a particular case. An example of a borderline case might be where some of the black section of the WHO probe shows, where there is no infection and it is difficult to decide on the source of any bleeding.

There are two relatively common surgical procedures that are used to treat periodontal disease. These procedures can be used when the disease has progressed beyond the point where scaling and polishing might provide a cure, or if scaling and polishing has proved unsuccessful as a treatment. These procedures come under the heading of 'periodontal surgery'.

The first procedure, known as 'gingivectomy' consists of totally removing the soft tissues of the gum which forms the pocket wall at the site of the disease. The purpose of gingivectomy is to eliminate the area between the tooth and the gum where tartar and plaque accumulate. Gingivectomy is likely to be used at Stage 3 when the pockets are only 'false pockets' and also probably after scaling and polishing has proved ineffective. Gingivectomy is not a suitable treatment for Stage 4 as too much root and tissue would be exposed if all the tissue forming the pocket was removed. One problem with gingivectomy is healing. The wound has to be specially dressed. Gingivectomy also leaves large parts of the root exposed and can cause problems with sensitivity and caries on the exposed roots. These problems now mean that gingivectomy is rarely used. It may well be that gingivectomy is not available as a treatment at some dental surgeries.

If Stage 4 has been reached then another relatively common procedure can be used. This procedure is known as 'flaps'. The basic idea behind the procedure is illustrated in Figure 12.6.

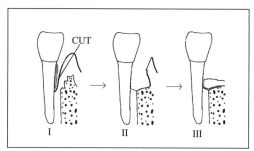

Figure 12.6

The first step of the procedure is to make a cut in the gum. The outside of the gum is then left as a 'flap'. Any diseased tissue is then removed and the affected areas of teeth and bones are given a smooth surface. The flap is then brought back into contact with the bone and teeth and kept in place with surgical stitches through the spaces between teeth onto the gum on the other side. The procedure is successful if the cut portion of the gum then adheres to the root surface of the tooth when the stitches are removed or are absorbed.

After this procedure the gum margin will be substantially lower than the original; some root as well as enamel may be exposed. The gum margin will, however, be much higher than using a gingivectomy for the same case. This procedure can have variations like adding bone grafts or using a skin graft instead of a flap.

Both gingivectomies and flaps can be very effective. They often allow patients to return to dental health with natural teeth remaining rather than progressing rapidly to extensive loss of teeth. In spite of this success rate, dentists find it much harder to 'sell' this procedure to patients. The necessity of work on teeth like fillings, extractions and crowns is much easier to understand than making cuts in gums. Explanations of what has to be done are also inevitably rather disturbing. The occurrence of these procedures in dental surgeries is therefore comparatively rare. Some dentists may not offer periodontal surgery and those that do will often be selective in their choice of patient. They will be looking for understanding of the procedures on the part of the patient and full co-operation in visits and aftercare. Anyone who has advanced periodontal disease may therefore have to exercise their own initiative if they want to try periodontal surgery rather than lose teeth. The details in this chapter will be vital knowledge for them. Patients might also be referred to a specialist for this procedure, especially if there are likely to be additions like bone grafts.

Dental professionals have given names to various specific types of periodontal disease that do not seem to fit the normal pattern. Two of these types will be discussed briefly.

The first of these is known as **'juvenile periodontitis'** and as its name suggests affects teenagers. This version of the disease affects the premolars and incisors initially, but then may spread to other teeth. A major difference from the normal version is that the gums may appear healthy, so that Stage 2 does not occur, but deep pockets and bone loss happen very quickly.

The second type is known as **'rapidly progressive periodontitis'**. This version affects people mainly between the ages of 20 and 40 years. As the name indicates the symptoms are similar to the version described in detail, but the onset and progression of the disease are very rapid to the extent that teeth can be severely affected within one or two years.

The treatment for these two versions is much the same as for the normal version. As noted earlier the basic cause of all periodontal disease is the action of certain bacteria. It is when these bacteria proliferate in-between the gum and the tooth that the disease takes hold. It is likely that both juvenile and rapidly progressive periodontitis are caused by external factors affecting the numbers and balance of bacteria. Control of both of these versions will also therefore depend on isolating and treating these external factors.

While these two versions of periodontal disease are rare, their existence does help to accentuate two points of general concern. The first point is that the susceptibility of people to periodontal disease can vary considerably. People with poor general health can often succumb to periodontal disease very quickly. As a consequence unhealthy gums can sometimes be a sign of other health problems. The second and related point is the need for every individual to monitor very carefully the condition of their mouth and to act on any changes. The details given in this book give readers certain aspects to look out for. In particular, for periodontal disease, readers should check the condition of the gums both in front of and behind the teeth and look out for any bleeding when using a tooth brush. Special attention is needed for the areas around bridges or dentures.

In relation to periodontal disease, unless either the individual or the dentist particularly looks for the symptoms, the disease can progress unnoticed for a period of several years. Bacterial imbalance, due to some external cause, can also happen to an individual at any time and then can cause a rapid progression of periodontal disease. Systemic diseases, such as cancer, diabetes, AIDS, or even malnourishment can all render the person more susceptible to periodontal disease.

Table of costs

The treatments covered in this chapter are carried out by an individual dentist or specialist. Complex constructions carried out in a dental laboratory are usually not needed. These two factors mean that costs are generally not as high as for teeth replacements. On the other hand, the treatment of extensive periodontal disease can take time, with as much as three hours needed in the dentists chair.

The figure for scaling and polishing varies because it might be more time-consuming if Stage 3 (Figure 12.3) has been reached. In this case very careful scaling under affected gums is needed and the procedure may have to be done in two or three stages. The figures given for gingivectomy and flaps are for the relatively straightforward cases that might be treated in a dental surgery. These figures depend on size of the operation, varying from just one or two teeth to a whole mouth that has to be treated.

The basis for the figures are given in Chapter 9. The figures in the table are for 1996 and are approximate to the nearest £. Where there are two figures, the top figure in each space is the minimum level of charge and the bottom figure is the maximum. The minimum figure is for routine work and is therefore the most likely figure that will occur.

Treatment	NHS	I	II	III	IV
Scaling and Polishing	6 15	15 45	20 60	25 75	30 90
Gingivectomy	20 140	33 200	50 250	60 300	80 400
Flaps	50 200	63 250	84 300	105 400	126 500

Chapter 13

Orthodontic treatment

for misaligned teeth

Summary level

The previous four chapters have all been concerned with treatment for the results of dental disease. By contrast this chapter is concerned with treating healthy teeth that are irregularly positioned in relation to the mouth and other teeth. Examples are teeth that protrude between the lips at rest, teeth that are crooked, and teeth that are obviously overcrowded. The branch of dentistry that is concerned with this type of problem is known as 'orthodontics'. Almost all orthodontic diagnosis and treatment is concentrated on one age group, namely late childhood and early teens, although all the treatments described can also be used with adults.

A few conditions and corresponding treatments in orthodontics are relatively straightforward and obvious. In many cases, however, there are difficult decisions to make about whether treatment should be given and what form this treatment will take. These decisions will involve three major parties; the young person, the parents and the dentist. In this case therefore both parents and potential patient really need to read the detailed level in this chapter, so that all procedures and implications for treatment are clear. A large part of the necessary interaction between parents and their son or daughter can then be resolved away from the dental surgery. Case Studies 2, 4 and 5 in Chapter 5 all involve orthodontic treatment and teenagers, so reading these may also help with family discussions.

If teeth are misaligned then the technical term for that condition is known as 'malocclusion'. The discussion in the detailed level starts with a description of the various kinds of malocclusion that can affect people at various ages and whether these need treatment or not. There are some malocclusions such as overcrowded or extra teeth that have to be treated for health reasons because they lead to inefficient biting and chewing and can become a site for disease. By far the majority of malocclusions are treated mainly to improve appearance, although the treatment may also have some effect on eating efficiency.

Dentists divide malocclusions into three classes, each of which has a different degree of impact on appearance and different possibilities for treatment. These three classes are described in the detailed level. A very common type of orthodontic treatment, which is most often applied to teenagers, involves moving teeth in their sockets. This process can take many months and needs the patient to wear an appliance. The details of possible appliances, how they work and what they entail in terms of treatment, time and costs are given in the detailed level. Some appliances are fixed and some can be removed by the wearer. Fixed appliances have to be checked on a regular fairly frequent basis by the dentist, while removable appliances require a consistent pattern of care and adjustment by the wearer. Different appliances can also have a different impact on appearance while they are being worn.

Decision-making on orthodontic treatment, by possible teenage patients and their parents, can be very difficult. The chapter concludes with a table of costs.

Detailed level

The way that teeth fit together is known as 'occlusion'. If some teeth are misplaced or irregular then the person is said to suffer from 'malocclusion'. The relationship of the jaws and the position and shape of teeth are inherited characteristics. If a parent has suffered from severely protruding top front teeth or overcrowding, then it is quite likely that their children will also have a similar problem. When dentists consider whether an orthodontic problem is serious enough to recommend treatment they place occlusions into three categories. The first category is called 'perfect' occlusion and is the occlusion generally accepted as looking best and being most efficient. It is estimated that under 10% of the population have perfect occlusion. If an occlusion is not perfect but is also not bad enough in the dentist's judgement to warrant treatment then it is called a 'normal' occlusion. If there are problems serious enough to warrant treatment the term 'malocclusion' is used. It is estimated that 60% of young people have malocclusion under this definition. This figure indicates that nearly all families with more than one child are likely to encounter a need to consider this area of treatment.

Some problems that come under the heading of malocclusion are relatively straightforward and need little decision-making. One example is where the young person has overcrowded or extra teeth, both quite common problems where very often the only treatment needed is extraction of particular permanent teeth. Also relatively straightforward are problems that are related to the change from first teeth to permanent teeth. First teeth can often be extracted at critical times in order to reduce the possibility of an orthodontic problem. Other problems are particularly likely to arise if the relevant first teeth are missing because of early extraction after tooth decay. All these potential problems should be monitored and discussed at the regular six monthly visits to the dentist that are necessary for this age group.

Unfortunately many of the situations and consequent decisions to be made in this area are not straightforward. Treatment for malocclusion can be necessary if the malocclusion is likely to cause excessive wear on teeth or the joints and muscles of the jaw, but this condition is rare. Malocclusion can be a factor in encouraging dental disease, but is almost always a far less important factor than the existence or non-existence of good oral hygiene. Malocclusion can also make some eating processes less efficient, but people with malocclusions can usually adjust eating techniques in order to minimise any potential problems. By far the major reason for treating most malocclusions is to improve appearance. Decision-making is therefore most likely to revolve around whether orthodontic treatment will improve the appearance of a young person. Such judgements are often subjective and the decision on whether orthodontic treatment is required can be difficult (see Case Study 5 in Chapter 5).

As will be seen in this chapter, most orthodontic treatment is a lengthy two-year process and needs dedication on the part of the patient. There can be a very tricky balance here between the necessity for treatment because of appearance and the prolonged trauma of the treatment. The young person concerned is at an age where appearance is a very important issue. The possibility of reaching adulthood with nice-looking teeth can be a very strong motivation for an 11 or 12-year-old. On the other hand, at this age young people are leading full and hectic lives with constant daily contact with their peer group. Orthodontic treatment often involves two years of wearing a rather ugly dental appliance. It may be that support will be given by some who are in a similar situation, but others might well make adverse comments and this possibility has to be understood and dealt with by the young person concerned. Success with such an appliance needs dedication in oral hygiene, care of the appliance and regular monthly visits to the dentist. The young potential patient has to understand the implications of this treatment and still be highly motivated to achieve success. The dentist is likely to check on the potential patient's motivation and attitude and the parental support they will receive before commencing orthodontic treatment.

To help with this decision-making it is useful to know how malocclusion is identified and how the levels of severity of problems are classified. These details are given next and are then followed by a description of the basis for treatment and details of the two most common types of appliance used for treatment. The chapter concludes with a table of costs.

A useful way of approaching definitions of malocclusion is to be clear about what is generally accepted as normal occlusion. Readers can probably understand the fundamental features of normal occlusion by thinking about the relationship of their own jaws and the positions of their teeth. For normal occlusion, if the teeth are brought together in their natural at rest position, the upper front teeth should fit snugly outside the front lower teeth and the back teeth should meet face to face. It is the relationship between the positions of the front teeth on the upper and lower jaws which often causes a major orthodontic

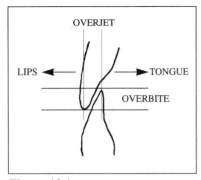

Figure 13.1

problem. The 'normal' situation for front teeth is shown in Figure 13.1.

In Figure 13.1 the distance between the two vertical lines is known technically as the 'overjet' and the distance between the two horizontal lines is known as the 'overbite'. The nature and size of the overjet is often a significant feature of an orthodontic situation that needs treatment. The presence of an abnormal overbite can affect the possibilities for treatment as sometimes an abnormal overjet cannot be treated satisfactorily without also treating the abnormal overbite. Dental professionals have grouped malocclusions into three classes. These classes will be described next as it can be helpful when contemplating treatment to realise the differences between types of occlusion.

Class I malocclusions occur where the basic relationships between the jaws and teeth are normal as described, but problems exist on one or both jaws with one or several teeth. Examples are overcrowding, or missing, misshapen or crooked teeth. Around 50% of the population has Class I malocclusion, although many of these will not be serious enough to warrant treatment. Treatment for Class I malocclusion is often straightforward and quick, extraction for overcrowding for example. Some Class I malocclusions will need orthodontic appliances to be fitted as described later in this chapter.

Class II malocclusions are concerned with the shape of the upper jaw and the way the front teeth incline as they grow out of that jaw. There are two basic types of Class II malocclusions. In the first type the upper front incisors are inclined forwards, sometimes to such an extent that they protrude from the lips at rest. The overjet in this case is very much increased. In the second type of Class II malocclusion the upper front incisors are tipped back. In extreme cases they are in contact with the biting edges of the lower incisors, so that the overjet is zero. Around 40% of the population has Class II malocclusion, but not all of these are serious enough to need treatment. Treatment for Class II malocclusion will almost certainly involve the wearing of an orthodontic appliance.

Class III malocclusions arise from the relationship between the upper and lower jaws. The upper jaw may be too far back, or the lower jaw too far forward. In extreme Class III malocclusions the overjet might be reversed, i.e. the upper incisors might fit behind the lower incisors. Around 15% of the population has Class III malocclusion. Class III malocclusions can be difficult to remedy.

Virtually all malocclusions are due to genetic factors. Premature loss of first teeth and a habit of sucking thumb or fingers that lasts into late childhood can cause Class I malocclusions. Malocclusions due to sucking habits will often correct themselves when the habit stops, as it usually does at puberty if not sooner. Apart from extraction, treatment for malocclusion normally involves altering the relationship of teeth to their supporting structures. Most commonly the teeth will be made to change their slope or incline by being made to rotate in a vertical plane in their sockets. Teeth may also be made to rotate in a horizontal plane in their sockets or, much more rarely, raised or lowered in their sockets.

Figure 13.2 illustrates what has to happen and problems that have to be overcome in order to change the incline of a tooth within its supporting structure.

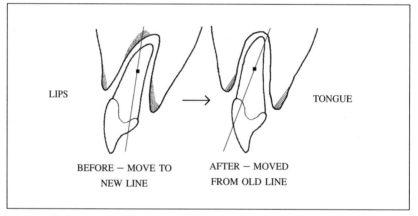

Figure 13.2

The purpose of the orthodontic treatment illustrated in Figure 13.2 is to rotate the tooth in a vertical plane in order to change its incline. In the 'before' section of Figure 13.2 pressure is applied to the tooth in order to make it move in the direction of the line. The 'after' section of Figure 13.2 shows the tooth in its final new position with a line indicating where it was initially. As one part of this process the bony part of the socket has to undergo quite radical changes. The sections of bone shaded with dots in 'before' have to disappear and the sections of bone shaded with lines in 'after' have to be made to grow.

The fact that there has to be bone loss and growth raises three issues as follows:-

1. Such changes in bone structure are much easier to achieve when the person concerned is young and bone structures are changing anyway because of growth factors.

2. Bone loss and growth can only be brought about by a steady constant

force. This force must not be too great as it would then cause damage or too small or it would be ineffective. It must be continuous, otherwise any stoppage would allow the bone structure to return to its previous state.

3. The bone changes have to be allowed to stabilise in their final position. This condition means that the orthodontic appliance has to stay in place for around six months after the teeth have reached their final position.

In mechanical terms an orthodontic appliance has to satisfy the second issue listed above in that it has to provide a steady constant force. In order to appreciate what has to be done it may be useful to consider the analogy of righting a tree trunk or pulling it out by its roots. One way of achieving these results is to attach one end of a cable fairly high up on the tree and the other end to a rigid structure like a rock face at or near ground level. The cable is then decreased in length, often just by using a hand-held device. The force produced gradually makes the tree change its inclination and will finally uproot it. Orthodontic appliances use the same principle. Stainless steel wires are joined between the teeth that are to be adjusted and to a fixed point or points. These wires are then shortened over a period of time. It is the size and direction of the force applied by the wires and the nature and continuity of the gradual changes that are applied over time that are crucial to the success of the process.

There are two types of orthodontic appliance in common use. One way of distinguishing the difference between these two types is to describe the first as 'removable' and the second as 'fixed'. There are some orthodontic problems that can only be treated using a fixed appliance, but for many of the most common orthodontic problems it is possible for a patient to have a choice of a removable or a fixed type of appliance.

In order to help readers to be clear about the issues involved in this choice, details are given about the way each type operates, the nature of the experience at the dental surgery and the ongoing personal care and maintenance procedures that the wearer has to follow. Included in these details are the advantages and disadvantages of the use of removable and fixed appliances.

Removable orthodontic appliances

These appliances are called 'removable' because the wearer can take out and replace the appliance, whereas 'fixed' appliances cannot be removed by the wearer. Removable appliances still have to be worn virtually all the time, including at night. The appliance needs to be removed and immediately replaced after every meal for cleaning and can be removed while the wearer is engaged in contact sport.

Removable appliances basically consist of a plate made of acrylic which fits into the mouth. Stainless steel wires are fixed to the plate and placed in contact with teeth. Some of these wire connections have fixed lengths and keep the plate in place while other wire connections are adjustable in length in order to change the incline of the relevant teeth.

Figure 13.3 is a diagrammatic illustration of a removable orthodontic appliance. It can be seen that the plate needed for a removable appliance has to be quite large. This size consideration normally means that removable appliances are most often used for teeth on the upper jaw where the plate will fit on the roof of the mouth. Removable appliances are not as easily fitted to the lower jaw as the plate must be small so that it does not interfere with the movement of the tongue.

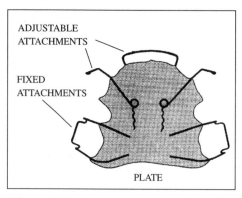

Figure 13.3

The plate for the removable appliance is kept in place by the wires that form the fixed attachments locking on to back teeth. The back teeth most commonly used for these fixed length attachments are the first molars (number 6 in Figure 7.2). Other wires, that can be adjusted for length, are then attached to the front teeth that need to be re-aligned. The adjustment of the length of the wires is usually done by a monthly visit to the dentist, but the appliance can have built in adjusters which have to altered by the patient once a week. Teeth are sometimes dealt with in sequence with the canines (number 4 in Figure 7.2) re-aligned first and incisors next. Very often teeth have to be extracted as a part of the treatment. Such extractions are usually made after the appliance has been worn for a short period of time. The appliance can also sometimes be replaced by a simpler version for the final period of six months of consolidation.

Removable orthodontic appliances are made in dental laboratories using specifications that are supplied by dentists. The fitting of a removable appliance will take two or three visits to the dentist. A full diagnosis of problems and possible remedies includes taking X-rays that show the positions of teeth and the relationships of bone structures in the head and jaws. Generating the specifications for the appliance will need plaster casts of both upper and lower jaws. These casts are obtained by asking the patient to bite on soft material which then hardens. Some people find this procedure unpleasant. During the first one or two visits the dentist will also discuss the nature of the treatment with the young person and parents in order to be reassured that the full implications of wearing the appliance as described in this book are understood.

Removable orthodontic appliances usually take from ten days to three weeks to be made at a dental laboratory. When the appliance is fitted for the first time the dentist will check that it is reasonably comfortable and that the wires are correctly positioned and at the correct initial lengths. The procedure for removing and replacing the appliance will be explained and practised by the patient. It is easy to damage the appliance or change the settings on the appliance by incorrect removal and replacement.

Removable appliances can feel bulky and uncomfortable, especially when they are first fitted. At an early stage they may also cause teeth some pain plus interference with normal speech and eating processes. Wearers will need time and patience to become acclimatised to the way that they feel in the mouth. It is easy for food particles to become lodged in between the appliance and teeth so the appliance needs to be removed after meals or snacks in order to clean both the appliance and the teeth. Some foods like sticky toffee can also cause extra problems. As explained earlier, the mechanical principles on which the appliance is based requires that the length of the wires needs to be adjusted on a regular and consistent basis. In order to make these adjustments the patient has to follow a very strict routine which will usually mean monthly appointments to see the dentist.

One advantage of removable appliances compared to fixed appliances is that they are relatively robust and can be easily replaced or mended. Removable appliances can also be removed for short periods of not more than two hours, in order to relieve discomfort or to play in contact sport. In terms of appearance, the only part of a removable appliance that is visible is the wire that runs across the top front teeth. The effect on appearance is therefore quite small. As already mentioned, the appliance does tend to feel obtrusive in the mouth and this symptom can make the wearer believe that the use of the appliance will also be very evident to others.

Fixed orthodontic appliances

A fixed orthodontic appliance consists mainly of brackets which are attached to teeth and a wire which joins the brackets together. This situation is illustrated in Figure 13.4 which shows a section which consists of one end of a fixed orthodontic appliance. The other end will be a reflection of this section with an end bracket on a back tooth on the other side of the mouth.

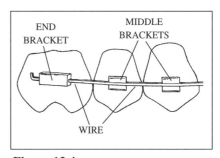

Figure 13.4

The mechanical principle for a fixed orthodontic appliance is basically the same as for a removable appliance. In this case, however, the wire is not gradually shortened in length at intervals by the dentist, but pull is exerted by springs or other elastic devices permanently attached to the device. The back teeth acting as the anchor points for the movement required. The general effect is still to alter the incline of the front teeth. If a change of inclination of front teeth on the upper jaw is all that is needed then a fixed appliance would be a direct alternative to a removable appliance. There can be additional features on a fixed appliance, for example, the fittings on individual teeth may not be just brackets. A crooked tooth may have a strap around it which enables that tooth to be rotated in the horizontal plane when force is exerted. In contrast with removable appliances, fixed appliances are equally suitable for upper and lower teeth.

The brackets of a fixed orthodontic appliance are fixed to the teeth by a process known as acid etching. This process is described in Chapter 9 on fillings. The brackets and wires of fixed appliances can be used equally effectively for upper and lower teeth. They can also be used to achieve more complex results than removable appliances. In general the appliance when fitted will have a much more complicated appearance than as illustrated in Figure 13.4. There may be more than one connecting wire and the springs producing the tension may also be evident. Fixed appliances are more comfortable to wear than removable appliances as there is no plate and no necessity of removal for cleaning. Fixed appliances are less robust than removable appliances. The main problem is that the brackets fixed to teeth can fairly easily become dislodged. A sharp blow or biting hard on the wrong kind of food can sometimes cause a bracket to lose its adhesion to the tooth.

All the work involved in fitting a fixed appliance has to be undertaken in the dentist's chair. This experience contrasts with receiving a removable appliance which is made in a dental laboratory and then subsequently fitted on the patient. As can be imagined, the construction and fitting of a fixed orthodontic appliance is a delicate and exact process which is also very time-consuming. It is very likely that patients will be referred to a specialist for fitting a fixed orthodontic appliance.

The procedure for fitting a fixed orthodontic appliance is likely to need between two and four visits to the specialist concerned. The first visit will be reasonably short, between 15 and 30 minutes, and will be concerned with taking precise details about the teeth and bone structures. Casts of the teeth and X-rays will be taken together with various measurements of relationships within the mouth. During this visit a decision is likely to be made about the actual nature of the appliance. This decision will be discussed with the young person and any accompanying parent. The actual fitting of the appliance may be done on one subsequent visit, in which case the visit could take up to one and a half hours. As an alternative the fitting of the appliance can be spread over two or three visits, but even in this case one of the visits is likely to last at least an hour. Parents might like to be present for this treatment session in order to provide support for their son or daughter.

When the fitting of the appliance has been completed, instructions will be given for the care and maintenance of the appliance. The first point to be made is that oral hygiene is an absolute priority, as there are so many extra places where plaque can accumulate. The cleaning of teeth and appliance together can be considerably more difficult than just cleaning basic teeth. It is especially difficult to clean between the appliance and the teeth. A special soft brush may be given to the patient for this purpose. Special wax may also be provided to coat a particular part of the appliance if it starts to cause soreness to mouth surfaces. The patient may also have to change or adjust on a regular basis the springs or other elastic devices that apply the force to the connecting wire. Instructions on what can and cannot be eaten and how to eat will also be given. Biting on apples and other possibly crisp or hard substances has to be avoided. Sticky toffee or any other substance that might adhere to the space between the appliance and the teeth must not be eaten. Any damage to the appliance, in particular a dislodged bracket, must be dealt with by a prompt visit. Contact sports either have to be stopped or a special gum shield has to be acquired and worn consistently.

The appliance is likely to cause discomfort to the affected teeth for the first twenty-four hours. Any discomfort lasting longer than twenty-four hours should be reported. The wearer of a fixed orthodontic appliance will also have to visit the specialist who fitted the appliance on a regular basis, probably once every month or two months. If this specialist is not their normal dentist then regular visits to their normal dentist must also continue on at least a six-monthly basis.

In some ways it is difficult to make comparisons by listing the advantages and disadvantages of removable and fixed appliances. Removable appliances are used more frequently than fixed appliances because they are more robust and easier to fit. One factor that might influence a decision to use a removable appliance is the personality and lifestyle of the potential wearer. If it is likely that the patient will not wear the removable appliance consistently then the young person, parent and dentist might want to consider the use of a fixed appliance. For many malocclusions, as for example when the lower jaw is involved, there is no choice and a fixed appliance is the only possible course of treatment. In terms of appearance, fixed appliances are more obtrusive than removable appliances but are more comfortable to wear, so causing less self awareness than removable appliances. The fact that fixed appliances can achieve more complex results also means that they are much more sophisticated in construction. This also means that there are more possibilities of faults developing.

There are other features related to wearing orthodontic appliances that need to be considered. One of these features is again a major aspect in terms of affecting the patient's lifestyle. In order to understand the background to this major aspect it will be useful to return to the analogy of uprooting a tree. In that analogy it was suggested that one end of the cable was anchored to an fixed object like a rock face with the other end fastened to the tree. In orthodontic appliances the comparable anchor is one or more back teeth. Quite evidently these back teeth are not immovable and when subject to force are likely to be displaced. If this displacement of anchor teeth is not a part of the treatment for the malocclusion then the patient has to be asked to overcome this displacement by wearing another appliance. This appliance is generally known officially as 'extra oral traction' and is also called 'headgear and whiskers'. Figure 13.5 is an illustration of such an appliance.

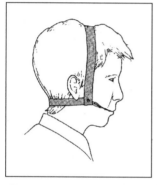

Figure 13.5

Extra oral traction works on the same principle of applying a force to the teeth. The 'whiskers' are wires which go into the mouth and are attached to the back of the appliance at each side of the mouth. The headgear consists of two straps which are attached to the wire. The anchor for the application of the force is the top and the back of the head. If extra oral traction is required then the headgear and whiskers will have to be worn for up to 12 hours each day. While it is only a small number of people (around 10%) receiving orthodontic treatment who will need extra oral traction, such a requirement could be another considerable factor for decision making.

The use of orthodontic appliances can carry other risks. In some patients the use of an appliance can make supporting structures lose their grip on the teeth. A consequence of this is a considerable risk of encouraging gum disease. This risk will increase if there are any problems with oral hygiene and consequent build up of plaque. In other patients the use of an orthodontic appliance can cause the roots of teeth to change their shape or to become absorbed in the supporting bone structure. The possibility of these problems again highlights the need for careful and consistent monitoring by the dental practitioner over the period of treatment.

The emphasis in this chapter has been on the treatment of young people, aged around ten to fourteen years. Older people, particularly those aged from eighteen to thirty, can also be treated for malocclusion problems. It may be relevant to use the general experience of such patients in order to emphasise the positive aspects of orthodontic treatment. For this older age group, they will be making their own decision that they want to change their appearance. The person concerned will then gain a considerable lift in terms of confidence and feeling of personal well-being when the treatment is completed. Motivation for wearing appliances and maintaining oral hygiene is not a problem with such adults. For younger people the same conditions apply with the same result very likely, although other factors may stop them seeing the positive benefits quite so clearly.

Table of costs

The costs of orthodontic treatment are quite high. However, if the patient is under 18 and is being treated as an NHS patient then the treatment will be free. The NHS figure in the table is therefore for adults.

A figure is given for preparation, which will be the same for both fixed and removable appliances. The figure for removable appliances is for each appliance. While some patients will only need one removable appliance other patients will require two and some may even need three or four appliances for their course of their treatment.

Fixed appliances are often fitted on both lower and upper jaws. The figure given is for a single appliance. If appliances are needed for both jaws then the figure is likely to be nearly double the figure given in the table.

The basis for the figures are given in Chapter 9. The figures in the table are for 1996 and are approximate to the nearest £. Where there are two figures, the top figure in each space is the minimum level of charge and the bottom figure is the maximum. The minimum figure is for routine work and is therefore the most likely figure that will occur.

Treatment	NHS	I	II	III	IV
Preparation	56	80	100	140	200
Removable per appliance	58	120 204	150 264	175 325	200 386
Fixed per appliance	70/160	200 800	250 1000	300 1200	350 1400

Chapter 14

Accidental damage

occurrence, treatment and prevention

A quick guide to dental first aid is given in Chapter 17, and if a reader has an urgent problem then they should refer to that chapter immediately.

Introduction

Accidental damage to the teeth and their supporting structures can of course happen to anyone, but it is a common problem for young people. About 1 in 10 children suffer such accidental damage by the time they are five, and by the time they are 15 one third of all young people have suffered such accidental damage.

When a person suffers an accidental injury of any kind it is vital to carry out correct procedures quickly in order to minimise long term consequences. If the injury involves the teeth or the mouth, there are some occasions when action has to be taken immediately, before contacting a dentist. It is also vital that any accident which might have involved the mouth should be followed by a visit to the dentist as soon as possible, even if there are no visible signs of damage. This chapter gives the essential background to understanding when action needs to be taken immediately and why a dentist has to be contacted urgently. After immediate problems have been dealt with by a dentist, there can be choices for restorative work that may be needed; details of such choices are given in this chapter. The chapter concludes with a short section on ways of preventing damage to teeth.

The detail given in this chapter is approached by identifying the nature of possible injuries and any possible long term effects. After a particular injury has been identified possible treatments for that injury are given by:- (1) describing any treatment that should be administered before contacting the dentist and (2) describing treatment that the dentist is likely to give in the short and long term in order to restore any damage. Case Study 3 in Chapter 5 is an example of treating the result of accidental damage to a tooth.

Initial procedure

The initial procedure for dealing with injuries that involve the mouth are the same as for any other kind of physical damage. The patient will need comfort and reassurance. If other injuries such as concussion or severe bleeding are also involved then they will often need priority. The subsequent action to be taken in relation to injuries involving the mouth depends on the nature of the injury. The main evidence for injury to the mouth is likely to be visible signs of damage or that the person feels pain. Visible signs of damage will include a tooth having a piece missing or with an obvious crack in the surface, or a tooth may be loose or even have been knocked out of its socket. If there are no visible signs of damage the tooth may still be severely damaged in the area below the gum. The supporting tissues may also be damaged, including those that provide the blood supply for the tooth. If any problem in this area is not investigated and treated in spite of the lack of any visible sign, the consequences can be severe. Pain may or may not be present for injuries that are not visible.

Nature of injuries and corresponding methods of treatment

For the dental profession injuries to the mouth come under the heading of 'dental trauma' and they use various ways of classifying injuries to the teeth and supporting structures in order to arrive at the correct treatment for a particular injury. One starting point for analysing the different types of injury is to look at two cases as follows:- (1) injuries that affect the teeth but not the supporting structures and (2) injuries where the tooth is not affected but the supporting structures are damaged. Many injuries will involve both of these cases in which case the treatments have to be combined.

Starting with the first case, an injury to a tooth but not the supporting structures and in order to discuss the various possibilities for accidental damage to teeth, it will be helpful to use Figure 14.1 (which is a repeat of Figure 6.1) for reference. In general the treatment for an injury to a tooth varies according to the position of the injury on the tooth and whether the pulp chamber has been disturbed or not.

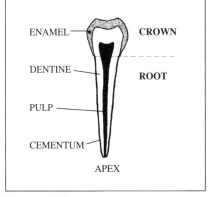

Figure 14.1

Injuries to the crown of a tooth are most common feature of any injury to the mouth. The four teeth at the front of the mouth are most likely to be involved (those numbered 1 in Figure 7.2). In most cases where it is just teeth and not the supporting structures that are affected, treatment at home is not needed except that no pressure should be applied on an injured tooth until the dentist has been seen; the tooth should not be used for biting or chewing.

There are three major possibilities for types of injury to an individual tooth evident from Figure 12.1. These are where damage is caused to:- (1) The enamel only, (2) The enamel and dentine, (3) The enamel and dentine and pulp.

The consequences of an injury to a tooth will also depend on the position of the injury; in general extended fractures that are near the crown (technically known as in the coronal third) are more difficult to treat. The position of the damage is important because of the need for support while a tooth goes through the natural process of healing. If the damage is well below the line of the gum then natural support is given in part by the structures of the tooth socket. If the damage is in the coronal third of a tooth then keeping that part of the tooth fixed while healing takes place is difficult.

The most common type of injury to a tooth in the coronal third is a complete fracture of a section of a tooth. Such a fracture may just involve the enamel but could also involve the dentine and the pulp. If it is just the enamel involved then treatment is easy and not particularly urgent, but if the pulp is exposed then treatment is needed very urgently before the pulp has a chance of becoming infected. If both enamel and dentine are affected and even if the pulp is not exposed treatment is still needed urgently. Apart from the level of pain, it is often difficult for the injured person or other non dentists to identify whether the pulp has been affected or not. There can be occasions when it is evident that only a small piece of enamel has been lost, in which case an urgent visit is not necessary, but normally when a piece of tooth breaks off it is sensible to seek an urgent appointment with a dentist. If possible it is also worth taking the broken piece to the dentist, even though replacing it is unlikely to be a realistic option.

If it is only the enamel that is fractured then the treatment depends on how much is broken away. A small amount missing may just need smoothing and reshaping with a power tool (see Chapter 8). If a relatively large piece has broken away then a surface filling will be needed and Chapter 9 on fillings is relevant. If the fracture involves the dentine or the dentine and pulp then treatment involves dressing the remaining section in order to stop infection, reduce pain and encourage healing. The necessity for an urgent appointment is very evident. The tooth will then be covered with a temporary cap which will stop it being used for eating so that it receives no pressure. After a period of about three months the tooth should have partially healed by producing more dentine and it is then likely to be possible to fit a permanent crown (see Chapter 10). If the pulp does become infected then the tooth can be treated by root canal treatment, a post and a crown (see Chapter 10).

Injuries to a tooth that occur well below the gum line can often be treated successfully even if the damage is quite severe. This success occurs because the broken pieces of a tooth can heal by rejoining in a similar way to broken bones, but as with bones this healing is only effective if the two adjacent fractured sections are not disturbed. While the tooth socket supplies some stability to the tooth, it is also necessary for the tooth to be held rigidly in place by a splint. Such splints are normally connected to other teeth and are also designed to stop the injured tooth receiving pressure during the eating process. Without such splinting the tooth is likely to deteriorate and can eventually become infected through the damaged section. Unfortunately not all damage that occurs below the gum gives obvious symptoms. This possibility of damage below the gum without symptoms is another reason why any blow to the mouth should be followed by a prompt visit to a dentist.

Complete healing of a permanent tooth damaged below the gum line is much more likely to take place when the person is a child or young teenager. This greater possibility of healing occurs because the pulp chamber and the gap in the tooth at the apex have a considerably larger diameter than for older people. Any rupture of the nerves or blood supply are therefore likely to have a much better chance of healing. It is therefore especially vital that parents take their children to a dentist as soon as possible after they receive any blow on the mouth.

The second possibility noted in the beginning of this chapter concerns an injury where the supporting structures of a tooth are damaged but the tooth remains totally intact. In this case it will be helpful to use Figure 14.2 (which is a repeat of Figure 6.2) for reference.

Two immediate points can be noted from this Figure 14.2. The first point is that the tooth can act as a lever so that any blow at the crown of the tooth will cause rotation about the centre of the tooth and a displacement of the apex. Such a displacement can cause the connections between the nerves and blood supply of the tooth to be severed. In an adult this disruption is very unlikely to heal. As even a slight blow can cause this disruption there can be little or no pain and the first sign will appear after a period of months when

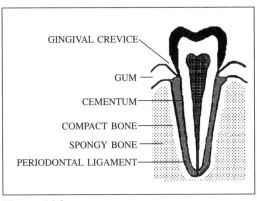

Figure 14.2

the tooth becomes discoloured. For children and young teenagers the space at the apex where the blood vessels and nerves run through to the supporting structures has a much greater diameter and healing is then possible. Such healing may be helped if the tooth is splinted. For such younger people an early diagnosis and treatment can make a big difference to the long term viability of the tooth. Again it is important to visit a dentist quickly if there is any possibility of an injury to the supporting structure of a tooth.

The other point that is evident from Figure 14.2 is that the severity of any damage to the supporting structures can be judged by which tissues are affected, moving from the periodontal ligament to the compact bone to the spongy bone. From the patient's point of view the tooth may be loose or even completely displaced from its socket. If the tooth is still in place then it should be disturbed as little as possible and a visit to a dentist or hospital must be treated as an emergency. The question of which tissues are affected is to some extent irrelevant as the treatment for each case is the same; the tooth needs to be held rigidly in place in its original position and all the tissues can then have a good chance of healing and restoring the viability of a tooth. As noted earlier, for adults the blood supply of a displaced tooth is not likely to be restored. The pulp of a displaced tooth will die and when the tooth is firmly fixed again it will need root canal treatment.

If a tooth is completely displaced from its socket it can be replaced, with a good chance of success, as long this replacement is done within one hour. Again the possibility of success is much greater for younger people. If an accident happens where it is possible to contact and reach a dentist quickly then that procedure should be followed. The tooth should be kept moist between the injury and delivery to the dentist by storage in the patient's saliva or in milk. If the accident happens in a remote place, or in other circumstances where reaching a dentist within an hour is not possible, then immediate replacement of the tooth in its socket can be the start of treatment which saves the tooth. The tooth should only be very quickly cleaned of any obvious foreign material and then should be reasonably firmly replaced in its socket in its original position. Contact with a dentist must be the next priority as the tooth will need to be held firm by a splint as soon as possible. The patient will have to be very careful not to disturb the tooth before arriving at the dental surgery or hospital.

If a permanent tooth is lost through injury then an artificial replacement will be needed (see Chapter 11). If a first or 'baby' tooth is lost, especially a back tooth, then the dentist is likely to fit a space retainer. The purpose of this device is to keep the remaining teeth properly aligned. As noted earlier in this book, first teeth normally act as a guiding structure for permanent teeth. Without the space retainer in position the erupting permanent tooth could become severely misaligned.

It is very important that any treatment for injury to teeth or their supporting structures should be monitored very carefully. Regular visits to the dentist on at least a monthly basis are likely to be necessary for a period of time up to one year after initial treatment for an injury to the mouth.

A blow to the mouth can cause severe damage where bone becomes fractured. One symptom of a particular type of fracture is that a group of three or four teeth move together in relation to the rest of the jaw bone. Such an injury will need urgent treatment in hospital.

Protection of teeth

Protecting the teeth from injury is mainly a question of taking two sensible precautions. The first is not to use the teeth for anything except eating. The teeth should not be used to crack nuts, open screw bottle tops or break thread for example. The second precaution is to wear a mouth guard for any participation in an activity where a blow to the mouth is a possibility. Particular examples of such activities are contact sports like football and sports which involve the use of a hard ball like cricket or hockey. Mouth guards, or gumshields as they are often called, are easily available from nearly all dentists. In order to supply a mouth guard the dentist will have to make an impression of the teeth and gums, which normally takes no more than five or ten minutes. The cost of such a guard is likely to be between £20 and £40.

Chapter 15

Other problems and Treatments

specialist help may be needed

Introduction

Most of the problems and treatments described in this chapter are encountered by very few people, probably less than one in a thousand. On the other hand, if readers or their friends or relations do need any of the treatments described in this chapter then the chapter could provide information that is difficult to obtain elsewhere. This chapter will then be of considerable assistance.

Many of the treatments outlined are likely to be given in a specialist dental practice, or in a dental hospital as a result of the patient being referred by their own dentist. Detailed cost estimates are not given in this chapter, as the infrequency of these treatments means that any kind of standard pricing is not available. Anybody having to pay for these treatments should ask for prior estimates in writing if possible. Some of the treatments described in this chapter are used as a part of a course of treatment for areas dealt with in the previous six chapters. One example is alveoplasty, which is surgery that is sometimes necessary to make the wearing of full dentures more comfortable. The description of that treatment is placed here rather than in Chapter 11 on extractions, bridges and dentures because very few people need this surgery. Placing a description of alveoplasty in Chapter 11 would obscure the main issues in that chapter which concern the great majority of people.

The detail in this chapter is approached through identifying problems and then giving associated treatments. In the previous six chapters the treatments in any individual chapter were all related to a particular theme like, for example, orthodontics in Chapter 13. In this chapter the problems and treatments are not related to a theme but are largely separate and distinct. The reader may therefore not be able to identify what is relevant for them quite so quickly, but in order to help with the process of finding relevant detail the names of treatments in this chapter are set in bold type. As an additional aid for helping readers look up problems and treatments in this chapter the details are divided into two sections. The first section deals with treatments placed under the heading of oral surgery. The second section discusses problems that have related medical or psychological factors. Dentists often have to diagnose and treat such problems, although co-operation with other health services is also often necessary.

Oral surgery

For the purposes of this chapter **oral surgery** is taken to mean any treatment where tissues on the inside of the mouth have to be cut. In some cases such treatments are relatively common and have been described already. Examples are gingivectomy and flaps, which are common treatments for periodontal problems and are described in Chapter 12. It is the cases where oral surgery is used for less common problems that are described in this chapter. These cases are approached by identifying the problem and then the possible treatment. All oral surgery will involve the use of either a local or a general anaesthetic.

The first type of problem to be considered is associated with extractions. The problem occurs when all, or some part of, a tooth is present in the jaw but not visible above the gum. If this problem occurs it is sometimes necessary to undertake oral surgery in order to remove the part of a tooth or the whole tooth concerned. Examples of such problems are where a tooth grows sideways and is then known as **'an impacted tooth'**, or where a **part of a root of a tooth has broken off** and remained in the socket during a normal extraction. The basis of the treatment for all of the problems of this type is the same. Overlying tissue, which can be both skin and bone, has to be cut back in order to gain access to the offending tooth or part tooth which is then removed. During this procedure gums will be cut in such a way that they can easily be re-attached, either by stitches or a special kind of plaster. Like all minor surgery there will be a period of a week or more after the operation when special care has to taken. Normally a follow-up visit within two weeks is also necessary. This procedure can obviously vary in difficulty and can require either a local or general anaesthetic.

There is another complication that can arise when upper molars and premolars are extracted (see Figure 7.2). The ends of the roots of each of these teeth are located at positions very close to the maxillary air sinus. Sinuses are cavities in bones of the face and the skull. Their purpose is to reduce the weight of the skull and to add resonance to the voice. The **maxillary air sinus** is connected to the nasal cavity and often becomes infected as a part of having a cold or flu. In this case the connection to the nasal cavity can also become blocked causing pressure and considerable pain. Infections from teeth can also infect these sinuses and sometimes during tooth extraction the thin layer of bone between the end of the root of the tooth and the sinus may be perforated. If this perforation does occur then the patient may notice fluid entering the nose after drinking or rinsing the mouth. Such perforations have to be closed in order to stop cross-infection. This closure is normally done by stitching the gum, although a larger perforation may need a more complex procedure.

Another problem which has to be treated with oral surgery is the presence of a **cyst** in the mouth. Cysts are an abnormal collection of fluid contained in a membrane separated from the surrounding tissue. Within the mouth they tend to occur where there are other abnormalities. At the apex of a dead tooth or around an impacted tooth for example. As untreated cysts continue to grow, they have to be removed in order to stop the gums swelling and possible interfering with surrounding structures. Whenever possible cysts are removed complete with their separate lining. The procedures for removing cysts is similar to removing tooth remnants.

A treatment associated with root canal treatment or endodontics is **apicectomy.** Reference to Figures 6.2 and 6.3 will illustrate the background to this treatment. An apicectomy consists basically of removal of the tip or apex of a root or roots of a tooth, then cleaning out the root canal and sealing the resulting space with filling. Access to the apex is gained by cutting back the gum as a flap and making a hole in the bone just above the apex. The bone will replace itself in time and the flap of gum has to be sewn back in place. An apicectomy is likely to be needed if root canal treatment has been tried and failed or if there is some reason why root canal treatment is not possible for a certain tooth. One example of the second case is if a tooth has a crown attached with a post (see Figure 10.3).

A procedure sometimes necessary when patients receive full dentures is **alveoplasty.** The alveolar process is the name for the supporting structures of the teeth. When all teeth have been extracted, the bony ridge that forms a large part of the alveolar process can be left with protruding bumps that would make the fitting of full dentures difficult or uncomfortable for the wearer. Alveoplasty is the name given to surgery that involves trimming the bone surface in order to make it smooth and even. The skin tissue above the bone has to be laid back and the bone trimmed with cutting and smoothing instruments. The skin is then stitched back into place. This process is also sometimes called **ridge preparation**. If a plate of bone has to be removed then the operation is known as an **alveolectomy**.

A similar type of oral surgery is known as **frenectomy.** A frenum is a section of a special type of fibrous tissue which attaches the tongue and lips to the underlying bone. There are several of these frenum in the mouth. It can happen that the tissue in a frenum grows into a shape that interferes with natural processes like speech or tooth growth. Sometimes also the shape of a frenum can be an obstacle to the fitting of dentures. In these case the frenum is trimmed and it is this process which is known as frenectomy. The process will be similar to an alveoplasty except that as the frenum is made of relatively soft tissue the trimming will be easier and involve different instruments.

Following extraction of teeth the usual way to fill gaps is to use a bridge or a partial denture. An alternative is to fit a false tooth to a **metal implant.** The basis of this procedure is illustrated in Figure 15.1.

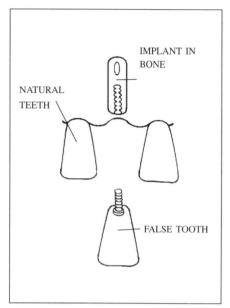

NATURAL TEETH

IMPLANT IN BONE

FALSE TOOTH

Figure 15.1

This treatment involves an artificial tooth being screwed into a plate that has been surgically implanted into the jawbone. These implants are made of either metal or a special ceramic material and have to be precisely designed in order to occupy the required space in the jawbone. Before the artificial tooth can be screwed and locked into place, the bone has to bond to the implant in a process known as 'osseointegration'. This process needs a period of three to six months to complete. Implants are a very expensive specialised treatment and the bonding process is not always successful. Implants are becoming more common but are still rarely used and many readers may not know of this possibility.

It is unlikely that an implant would be offered as a treatment for the case of a straight replacement of one missing tooth as illustrated in Figure 15.1, unless there was some pressing reason why a bridge would not be suitable. On the other hand, if an implant in such a case is successful, then it will seem much more natural to the wearer than the possible alternative of a partial denture or a bridge. The result is the same as a crown but does not require the presence of some of the natural root of the tooth. It could be that some readers might like to investigate this possibility following an extraction; it is another example where knowing of the possibility does give a choice of treatment.

Implants using osseointegration are most often used after injury or disease when other teeth or supporting tissues are not viable as supports for bridges or dentures. The implanted section can have magnets or other precision attachments (see Chapter 11) which can be used for locking dentures into place. See Case Study 11 in Chapter 5 for an example of implants used in this way.

Related medical or psychological factors

Moving on to problems that have **related medical or psychological factors,** dentists can sometimes treat these problems and are often able to diagnose the presence of more wide-ranging problems through observations on the condition of a patient's mouth.

The problems considered in the second section of this chapter are divided into three groups. This grouping has been done in order to help readers find the detail on problems of particular interest to them. For the first group the problems give symptoms that are generally located only within or around the mouth but are not normally associated with the condition of teeth. A relatively common example of such a problem is mouth ulcers. Other symptoms dealt with in this group include white patches, blisters, excessive dryness or considerable swelling. The second group consists of problems that affect the mouth and sometimes the teeth, but where the cause of the problem is frequently psychological rather than physical. Very often the main symptom in this case is pain, though grinding of the teeth at night can also be a consequence of a psychological problem. The third group consists of five general medical conditions that can generate symptoms in the mouth. These conditions are glandular problems, indigestion, cancer, bone disease and damage due to accidents or birth defects.

From the point of view of the patient the symptoms for mouth problems not directly related to teeth come under the three general headings of 'appearance', 'pain' and 'dryness'. Many of the conditions covered in this section also come under the general heading of **'stomatitis'.** Stomatitis is the overall name given to any inflammation of the lining of the mouth. Mouth ulcers are a condition that comes under this heading. The main indication of the presence of problems under the heading of stomatitis is appearance, although the areas concerned are also likely to be sore, especially when touched. The skin on the inside of the mouth is known as the 'oral mucosa' and this term will be used in order to note changes when problems occur.

In the first group, the existence of **mouth ulcers** is very clear as the normal even surface of the oral mucosa is disturbed by the presence of circular or oval patches. The interior of these patches has an obviously different texture to the normal mucosa. Mouth ulcers can also cause pain especially if they come in contact with harder items of food, like nuts or apples. Mouth ulcers are usually caused by the oral mucosa being broken or injured in some way. This injury can happen by biting or by contact with a rough edge on a tooth. As well as the type of mouth ulcers caused by injury, about one person in four suffers from a recurrent form of small mouth ulcers. Another factor which can either cause mouth ulcers, or prolong the time they last, is stress. Some people seem to be particularly liable to suffer from ulcers. The pastilles for treating mouth ulcers available from chemists can be a useful treatment. If mouth ulcers do not disappear within two or three weeks then they could be a symptom of a more serious problem and an appointment should be made to see a dentist.

Another symptom that is concerned with appearance is the existence of white patches on the oral mucosa and/or the tongue. There are three relatively common conditions associated with this symptom. The first of these conditions is known as **'thrush'**. With thrush the patches are soft and creamy-yellow and can easily be wiped off the mucosa. The mouth can also be sore. Thrush is caused by an organism called 'candida albicans' which is normally present in most healthy mouths. It only causes an infection when there is a disturbance in the normal balance of organisms in the mouth. This imbalance can be due to taking drugs for other general diseases. Thrush also occurs fairly frequently in young babies. Thrush is generally cured by treating the cause rather than the symptom, but lozenges can be prescribed that will reduce the patches and stop soreness.

White patches that cannot be wiped off are generally caused by an increased amount of a substance called 'keratin' on the surface of the oral mucosa or tongue. Such patches are called **'leukoplakias'** which is the second condition to be considered. Leukoplakias can be caused by many different factors or diseases. As some of these conditions are serious and can include cancer, it is again sensible to seek advice if they persist.

Another cause of white patches on the oral mucosa is a serious but relatively rare disease call **'lichen planus'**. Lichen planus affects other areas of skin besides the oral mucosa. It is a disease that mainly affects people of middle age or over and women more than men. The cause is unknown but it seems to be associated with depression and chronic anxiety. If this disease is not treated it will continue to cause unpleasant symptoms for twenty or more years.

The third change in appearance which is a symptom of problems is the presence of **blisters**, which have the scientific name of **vesicles.** Blisters on the lips are often called 'cold sores' and are usually a symptom of the person having the herpes simplex virus dormant in a facial nerve. This virus can be reactivated by sunlight or by another infection such as a cold. Blisters inside the mouth can be caused by taking food or drink at too high a temperature, but they can also be caused by more serious conditions like a blockage in the salivary glands. Blisters can also sometimes break down to leave mouth ulcers. Once again an appointment should be made if symptoms persist.

A **dry mouth** can be a very distressing symptom. The more or less constant production of saliva is a necessary part of digestion and an important factor in preserving the correct balance of organisms in the mouth. If the production of saliva is poor, or is easily lost through evaporation, then the person feels discomfort and possibilities of disease increase.

A dry mouth can be caused by local factors such as mouth breathing or excessive smoking. There can also be a direct cause such as blockages or diseases of the salivary glands. Other possible causes include chronic anxiety and the effect of certain drugs. A dry mouth can also be part of a general dehydration brought on by various causes. Unless the cause is evident and the condition is temporary anybody experiencing a dry mouth should seek help.

Infection in the **lymph nodes** in the neck is another problem which shows itself through appearance and pain. This problem is often called 'swollen glands'. The lymph nodes normally swell and become painful as a result of infection somewhere in the surrounding tissues and these symptoms can sometimes be the first sign of a problem.

Psychogenic disorders is the name given to problems where the patient feels pain but where the symptoms are believed to be caused by psychological problems like chronic anxiety and stress rather than having a direct physical cause. There are several psychogenic disorders which give rise to pain only in the area of the mouth and so might cause the person to go to a dentist. A fairly common problem of this type is known by the long name of **'temporomandibular pain dysfunction syndrome'**. The pain in this case is felt in the joint just below the ear that connects the upper and lower jaw. The name of this joint is the temporomandibular joint, hence the name of the disorder. Other symptoms of temporomandibular pain dysfunction syndrome include clicking in the joint and difficulty in opening the jaw any significant distance. This problem mainly affects women between the ages of twenty and forty. It seems to have no physical cause and usually stops after a period of time without any treatment being necessary. Problems in this joint can be caused by physical problems or diseases, so it is important to see a dentist if pain is felt and persists beyond two or three weeks.

There are two other sets of symptoms which occur in some patients where usually no physical cause can be found. For one of these the patient complains of a persistent burning sensation in the mouth and in the other the patient complains of a persistent dull pain, mainly over the upper jaw. Both of these sets of symptoms are most commonly reported by older women. It is important that anyone suffering from these symptoms for more than three weeks should see a dentist. Any possible physical cause can then be investigated and the dentist can then refer the patient for further appropriate treatment.

Another psychogenic disorder is called **trigemina neuralgia**. This disorder also causes pain in the facial area, but in this case when the disease is fully developed, the pain is triggered by touching a particular part of the face. The pain is short-lived but excruciating. As early symptoms vary, this disease can be difficult to diagnose. Once correctly diagnosed it can usually be treated successfully.

There is another kind of psychogenic disorder where the person concerned damages their teeth through actions brought about through habits arising from reaction to stress. The major example of this type of problem is compulsive grinding of the upper and lower sets of teeth together. This grinding mostly takes place when the person is asleep. This particular condition can cause considerable damage to the teeth. While the most effective cure is likely to be the removal of the cause of the stress, a dentist can take measures that reduce the damage. Occasionally such measures also stop the activity. One such treatment that helps to reduce damage is to identify and remove any contact points within the occlusion. Such points provide a subconscious focus for the grinding activity. The patient tries to 'grind them out' at night. Another treatment is to provide a 'night-time bite guard' which is similar to a sports gum shield.

Five other general medical problems that can involve a dentist in their treatment are described next. From the reader's point of view the major difference with these problems is that the symptoms will be obvious and action will already have been taken. The brief details given are therefore just for information.

The first general area that can cause problems in the mouth is **disorders of glands**, the salivary glands in particular. The salivary glands can become diseased through infection or blocked by stones formed through calcium deposits. Symptoms can include dryness, soreness and pain, blisters and ulcers. Treatments can include the use of drugs and minor operations.

Chronic indigestion can also cause problems in the mouth because it often generates a significant build-up of acid in the mouth and so leads to a deterioration of the teeth, gums and oral mucosa. If the indigestion is not causing too much pain and lasts over a period of years then deterioration of the condition of the teeth may be the first noted result of the problem.

Cancer of the lips, tongue and oral mucosa is rare in the UK. It can be caused by smoking and can follow other conditions of the mouth or cancers in other parts of the body. As with any cancer, it is early recognition of change in normal physical attributes by the person, followed by a diagnosis by an expert, that is essential in order to be able to treat the disease at an early stage. The possibility of a cure is then very good. Many people suffer occasionally from ulcers, lumps and other sore places in the mouth. It is when such problems last for longer than two weeks that action needs to be taken by the person concerned. Examination by a dentist will then soon establish whether such problems are due to more common factors like gum disease or a rough edge to a tooth. The dentist can then refer the patient to a hospital if necessary. Visiting a dentist on a six month checkup basis also provides a guard against serious oral problems.

Another part of the mouth structure which can cause problems is the **bones, muscles, ligaments and joints** associated with the mouth. These tissues can become diseased and can also suffer accidental damage. Such problems are often first identified during dental visits and treatment.

The last general problem concerns people who have **misshapen or damaged mouth structures** such as a hare lip or cleft palate. These problems can arise from birth defects or subsequent accidents or disease. While most of the treatment for such problems is likely to involve plastic surgery, a dentist will often have to provide dentures of some kind. In these cases a hole in the roof of the mouth is often filled with a device attached to the plate for the denture. This device is known as an 'obdurator'.

Chapter 16

Newer Treatments

how they can help,
who supplies them

Introduction

The main purpose of this chapter is to inform readers about some of the newer dental treatments becoming available. While this chapter is included mainly for interest, it is possible that some readers may be offered these newer treatments. Another possibility is that the details given here will motivate some readers to seek out dental practices that offer these newer methods and processes.

There are three general points about the nature of change in dental care that might help readers appreciate the way that these newer treatments could affect their own situation.

The first point is that the introduction of new treatments is a very slow process in general dentistry. This very slow uptake of change is partly due to the way that dentists are paid, particularly under the NHS scheme. The amount of money they receive is related to the number and classification of treatments administered. This method of payment means that introducing new and more expensive procedures is often difficult to justify on a cost benefit basis. Another reason for the slow take-up is that dentistry tends to be a rather conservative profession. What follows from this first point is that it is only a tiny proportion (well under 1%) of dental practices that are likely to have newer treatments and innovative procedures in place. This scarcity also means that it could well be difficult for an individual to find a dental practice that offers newer treatments. If asking your present dentist does not produce results, then using the information and contact points given in the later part of Chapter 17 might be helpful.

The second point is in a way more interesting from the point of view of this book, in that a major purpose of many of the suggested changes is to try to involve the patient more in the decision making process about problems and treatments, and also to try to make dental treatment a much more relaxed experience. This second point will be referred to again in the subsequent details given in this chapter.

The third point is that readers should be aware that some possibilities, such as implants, have already been discussed in Chapter 15. The use of implants is certainly an innovative treatment, but is not likely ever to be offered as a common procedure in your local dental practice. This chapter is particularly concerned with changes that might occur in general dental practices.

In general there are two connected factors that lead to changes in dental treatment: (1) the introduction of new technology, and (2) the results of research into dental treatment. It is difficult to discuss possible changes in any sort of order, but one of the new technologies that has made most impact outside of dentistry is computers, so advances that are connected to the use of a computer will be discussed first. Other possibilities will then be discussed in a random order.

Details

The main reason why computers are useful in the work place is that they can handle large amounts of data very quickly and efficiently. For a computer it makes little difference if this data is in the form of words, numbers or pictures. The computer can also be programmed to operate outside devices like robots, or more particularly in dentistry, machines for cutting and shaping materials. In this second case, the cuts and adjustments can be based on dimensions obtained from the data stored as pictures in the computer's memory.

The most common route for the introduction of computers into any new field is to start by using them for processing information like customer and stock records and then to proceed to more sophisticated uses like reading bar-coded prices or controlling robot-type devices. In some ways dentistry is following similar lines. Dentists are now allowed to keep patient records, appointments and bills, NHS returns etc. on computer and there are several suppliers of software that enable dentists to use computers for this purpose. In 1996 an estimate of dentists using computers for record keeping put the figure at no higher than 20-30%. From the patient's point of view a very much more interesting use of computers in dentistry starts from their ability to handle data in the form of pictures. Such a use of computers is sometimes called 'image processing' and it is this that will be discussed next.

Some particularly interesting applications of image processing related to dentistry are based on a device known as an 'intraoral camera'. The basic idea of this device is to replace the dentist's use of mirrors, overhead lighting and sometimes extra lenses on spectacles for examination of a patient's mouth, by a special probe that goes into the mouth and which transmits pictures to a TV type screen. Besides going to the TV screen the images can also be sent to and stored on a computer. From the point of view of this book, it is interesting to note that the main benefit reported by dentists who are using this device is that the patient can also see the TV screen and therefore see exactly what the problem is. The result of this joint viewing is that the patient is more able to be involved in discussion and will also realise the necessity of a course of treatment. In some cases the results of X-rays can also be seen on the same screen, which provides another aid to diagnosis and discussion.

Once images produced by the camera or X-rays are stored on the computer they can be processed in various useful ways such as concentrating on and 'blowing up' a small section of an original image, or lightening or darkening the shading in an image. The first could enable concentration on a particular trouble spot like a small cavity, the second could help to check on the position and the site of infection. Computers can also control external devices. It is particularly interesting that the main dental treatment that is replaced by this application is the use of amalgam or composite fillings, although at a considerably increased cost. In order to carry out this particular treatment the dentist has to prepare the tooth for a filling as usual. The intraoral camera is then used to scan the resulting cavity. The computer then uses the dimensions resulting from the scan to activate a cutting machine that produces a porcelain filling that exactly fills the cavity. The dentist then cements this filling into place. It should be realised that the part of process, where the computer controls the making of the filling, only takes two or three minutes, so the whole treatment can usually easily be fitted into a half-hour appointment like a 'normal' filling using amalgam or composite. Porcelain fillings are very hardwearing so the treatment usually has a very good prognosis.

Returning to the theme of trying to make the patient experience more relaxed, the two factors that probably cause most patient anguish are pain (or the possibility of pain) and sound. The sound is largely derived from the process of removing materials and shaping cavities. In old-fashioned terms the idea of a dentist's drill or the modern equivalents, airotors and handpieces which are in general use now (see Chapter 8). There are two new devices which can be used for carrying out the removing and shaping process. These devices have the additional benefit of being almost totally silent. The use of these devices also causes comparatively less pain and so more patients can be treated without the use of anaesthetics through injections.

The first of these devices is known as a KCP system, where KCP stands for 'kinetic cavity preparation'. This device works by ejecting a narrow band of minute particles of alpha alumina at a very high speed. In order to visualise the way a KCP works you should think of it as spraying away decay and shaping material, rather than the grinding process carried out with an airotor or handpiece. An everyday comparison might be the introduction of aerosols which can be used to cut and shape wood rather than having to use saws, files and sandpaper. The second device is a laser, which works by directing a narrow beam of very high intensity light. The dental application of lasers is again to remove and shape tissue, they are particularly helpful for fine work. This means that for small cavities, with small holes in the enamel, there will very often be no need to enlarge the hole in the enamel, which is obviously beneficial in not causing more damage. KCPs cost around £15,000 while lasers cost £30,000 or more, so KCPs are more commonly seen, but even then are relatively rare in general practice. Neither KCPs or lasers can be used on old amalgam fillings or to prepare large cavities. This limitation means that most dentists will still have to use airotors and handpieces for some of their work. This fact of partial rather than universal possibilities for use is another factor that can inhibit dentists from buying these devices.

While many innovative treatments are related to technology, some dentists are also using other techniques in order to try to improve the patient experience. One such technique is relaxation therapy or at a higher level, hypnosis. Relaxation therapy can be especially helpful for people who find the intrusion of fingers and objects in the mouth distressing. One particular example is people who 'gag' when the dentist tries to take impressions of their teeth in order to make crowns or dentures. It may well be worthwhile for such people to seek out a dentist who can administer relaxation therapy as an aid to particular aspects of treatment. Hypnosis may also be the only solution for people who cannot cope with any kind of anaesthetic procedure.

Two other aspects of treatment which patients often find unpleasant to experience or anticipate are injections and gum tissue being cut. Both of these have more technologically advanced replacements for present methods. 'Electronic anaesthesia' can replace injections and 'electrocautery' can replace the use of surgical scalpels.

Electronic anaesthesia is administered by placing a pad inside the mouth and sometimes another pad on the back of the hand. The patient is then given a device to hold in one hand and with the other hand they can activate a control on the device either under the dentist's instructions or as soon as any pain is felt. Activating the control generates 'waves' which stop the nerves in that area from working effectively. This means that pain messages are not sent to the brain. Some patients will have a 'tingling' effect in the area below the pad in the mouth and there are a very small number of people for whom the treatment is ineffective, but in general from the patient's point of view there are three main advantages to this system: the patient does not have to experience the slight pain and unpleasant feeling associated with receiving injections; the patient has some control over minimising pain; and there are no after-effects as there are with injections. Dentists who have used electronic anaesthesia report that their patients find it a very big help in making treatment more pleasant and so less stressful. This again ties in with the idea of having more relaxed patients.

The instrument used for electrocautery replaces normal scalpels and to some extent the use of heavy dressings. The most common kind of treatments electrocautery applies to are those related to periodontal disease as described in Chapter 12. Electrocautery basically provides a method of cutting soft fleshy tissue and sealing it at the same time. Even with electrocautery there will normally be some bleeding, but certainly much less bleeding than after using a normal scalpel. Even this aspect of the use of electrocautery will provide a less traumatic experience for the patient. There is an additional bonus for the patient, which is that either no dressings will be needed on the wound, or the amount of dressings and the length of time they will have to be in place will be very much reduced. The overall experience for the patient from the use of electrocautery is therefore considerably less unpleasant than the use of the more traditional methods.

The account of newer treatments given in this chapter only covers a small proportion of the possibilities being considered worldwide. Other relatively common suggestions include coatings for teeth that make them impervious to caries attack, and many different kinds of replacements for fillings and filling materials. It is likely that dentistry and the general care of teeth will change considerably as we approach the twenty-first century. Future editions of this book will reflect these changes.

Chapter 17

Personal dental care

dental first aid, sources of information

Introduction

This chapter has three main sections. The first section discusses ways in which individuals can help themselves and their families to keep in good dental health, the third section deals with dental first aid, and the second section gives points of contact if there are problems or if more detailed information is required. If someone has a dental emergency then they should go to the first aid section on page 140.

It is most likely that people reading this book will already be taking pains to keep in good dental health. In order to do this they will be using some of the products that are heavily advertised on TV and in magazines. The frequency of such advertisements illustrates the fact that these products are widely used and generate business worth over £200 million each year. The fact that a large proportion of the population has established regular personal routines for dental health is one reason why the national picture is one of continual improvement. Unfortunately not all individuals are a part of this improving picture, as illustrated in some of the case studies. From the personal point of view, it has to be realised that if an individual wishes to be a part of this improving picture then they do have to take positive steps. These positive steps and other aspects of home care are discussed under the four headings: **Lifestyle and habits, Diet, Day-to-day home dental care, Working with your dentist.**

The **Dental first aid** section contains some general advice, which includes suggestions for a dental first aid kit and what to do about holidays. The main part of this section is a list of twelve types of dental problem where home first aid might be a possibility.

The third section concerns **sources of information** and is aimed at two different sets of readers. The book is mainly designed to be used by individuals and families, but it will also be used in libraries and schools as a reference book for young people when they need to learn more about mouths and dentistry. The information sources are therefore discussed under the two headings: **Contacts for choice and complaints, Contacts for further information.**

Personal dental care

Lifestyle and habits

Many of the case studies in Chapter 5 demonstrate that, to a very large extent, the state of a person's teeth and gums depends on their lifestyle and habits. With a lifestyle that includes the wrong kind of diet, and without regular daily care of teeth and gums, dental problems will soon arise and rapidly become serious. On the other hand everybody has plenty of other daily concerns. Fitting time-consuming dental care activities into a busy schedule can seem unnecessary on occasions and can sometimes become totally neglected. People can also be overwhelmed by all the rather boring detailed advice about what you should do and not do for health reasons as a part of your lifestyle and habits. This advice seems to cover nearly all aspects of living including smoking, drinking, working, exercise and other leisure activities. The emphasis in this book is on choice. In the area of dental care people have a choice of diet and what they do about taking care of their teeth and gums. The choice will depend on their lifestyle and it seems sensible to try to plan dental care so that it fits into that lifestyle without too many problems. Two particular examples of choices which can fit into most lifestyles are: (1) to learn an efficient way of cleaning teeth and to then use that method after breakfast and before going to bed; and (2) to always book the next six months routine visit to the dentist when you finish a current course of treatment and before you leave the dental practice. Even if you cannot eventually make that particular day and time the reminder of the need for a check-up is there. The sections that follow give details of particular aspects of self-help but try to keep these to a minimum and where relevant to indicate how they might fit into different habits and lifestyles.

Diet

Probably the most critical aspect of diet is the role of refined sugar in causing the disease caries (or tooth disease). This role is described in detail in Chapter 6 and that description includes the reasons why it is the frequency and length of duration of sugar presence in the mouth rather than the amount of sugar that is the main factor in accelerating the progress of caries. Habits that include eating or drinking sweet things every half hour or particularly in the last hour before going to bed are bad news for healthy teeth. For healthy teeth you should not keep sweets in the car to suck when driving, or have sweetened hot drinks every hour and before going to bed, or give young children sweets every time they cry. Choosing non-sugar sweeteners, particularly in drinks, can alleviate this problem to some extent. Unfortunately sugar is present in many other foods in order to make them palatable or to improve their consistency. Even many substances that have a 'clean' or 'healthy' image such as mints and muesli bars often contain a considerable amount of sugar. Case study 1 in Chapter 5 is a clear illustration of how first teeth can be badly affected by an over-frequent sugar intake. Parents need to be very aware of possible problems and try to generate non-sugar habits even before their baby has any teeth.

Lifestyles and eating habits are very closely related and enjoying what you eat and drink is an important part of living. Although frequent sugar presence is bad, it is silly to go overboard on always rejecting sugar. Eating chocolates twice a week is not likely to do too much harm. On the other hand, eating fresh fruit and vegetables every day helps to keep healthy teeth and gums as well as aiding digestion and maintaining a correct vitamin balance.

Day-to-day home dental care

It is the products associated with day-to-day home dental care that are the subject of most of the advertising on TV and in magazines. The other aspect of dental care that is strongly featured in advertisements is care and fixing of dentures. The resulting advertisements are therefore mainly for: toothbrushes, toothpastes, mouth washes, plaque disclosers, dental floss, electric toothbrushes, cleaning agents and fixatives for dentures. Any chemist or large food store will also have many shelves full of personal dental health products. This is one area where everybody is faced with a considerable range of choices.

The reasons why day-to-day care for people with natural teeth is important were established in Chapter 6 and the main message is that teeth need to be cleaned regularly in order to stop the build-up of plaque and to remove food debris. The cleaning should also be done in a way that reduces the likelihood of gum disease. Dentures also need cleaning on a regular basis and the denture-bearing surfaces of the mouth need to be rested on a daily basis. For the very best results in reducing problems with natural teeth, every surface and crevice should be thoroughly cleaned immediately after any eating and drinking, especially if these involve a sugar intake. The method of cleaning should not be likely to cause erosion on tooth surfaces or encourage gums to recede. Referring back to lifestyles and habits, it should not be too difficult for most people to clean their teeth morning and night. The night clean has added importance because saliva is produced in much less quantity during sleep and so the healing function saliva produces (as described in Chapter 6) becomes much less effective. It is important therefore that any traces of sugar are removed before going to bed. After reading the recommendations for cleaning teeth in this section, you will be able to make a comparison with your present habits for home dental care. It is certainly true that regular cleaning of any kind, even only once a day, with a fairly new toothbrush and a well-known brand of toothpaste will make a considerable difference to the level of personal dental health compared to no cleaning at all. Another common and useful practice is to use a toothpick to remove food particles when these cause discomfort when lodged between teeth. Increased frequency, good brushing technique and use of other cleaning aids are all likely to add to the benefits obtained.

Using a toothbrush to clean teeth effectively is a skill, similar in some ways to using a can opener or a tennis racquet or, at a higher level, driving a car. For all these skills you eventually need to be able to perform them at a subconscious level. In order to achieve a good performance at a non-thinking, subconscious level, the skills must first be taught and practised at a thinking level, where the brain is actively concerned with how to handle the device and what positions are needed for its effective use. For playing tennis and driving a car the skills are usually very carefully taught by experts. Unfortunately for cleaning teeth very few people receive expert coaching in the correct physical actions. Such coaching, followed by practice under observation by a dentist or dental hygienist, is certainly the best option. All that can be done in a book such as this is to indicate some of the basics for a good technique and to suggest that some readers might find it beneficial to change their teeth-cleaning technique after checking their present habitual method. You may well be using an efficient method which differs from the one described here. There are many different and equally efficient techniques. If you do think that your method could be changed for the better, then you will need to clean your teeth, with the new technique, at a conscious level for a week or so in order to make the new technique habitual.

As a start your toothbrush should be a reasonable size, comfortable in the mouth, not too big and with medium tough bristles. The ends of the bristles should also be rounded rather than sharp. Any well-known toothpaste will be effective, fluoride and other additives can be helpful and flavoured toothpastes are a matter of individual taste. Many people use too much toothpaste. Around a centimetre or just under half an inch is enough.

By far the most important aspect of cleaning technique is to be methodical, to make sure you follow a route that covers every tooth and when you are at places on this route, to have techniques that deal with every surface, plus the spaces between teeth and, very importantly, the gap between the teeth and the gums (the gingivical gap, see Chapter 6). Figure 17.1 illustrates what is meant by having a route for cleaning teeth.

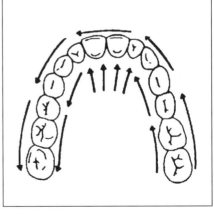

Figure 17.1

This figure indicates a route to take by following the arrows, starting at the front on one side, working round to the same position on the other side, then following the same route at the back of the teeth. These routes should apply to both upper teeth and lower teeth. Another feature of Figure 17.1 is that there are five arrows for the front of the teeth which can be taken to indicate five separate positions to work on with a corresponding five positions at the back of the teeth. These positions can be a useful guide to the idea that each position, which has not more than three teeth, has to be cleaned thoroughly before moving on. At each position there should be a sequence of two or three separate actions as follows: (1) a sideways, to-and-fro, movement to remove plaque and debris from the teeth, the spaces between teeth, and the gap between the teeth and the gums. This movement should be done with the brush at an angle of 45 degrees to the tooth as in Figure 17.2; (2) a rolling movement starting with the brush in position as in Figure 17.2, then taking the bristles with a rolling motion from the gum to the biting and chewing surface of the tooth. This will then flick the loosened debris away from the tooth. (3) for back teeth the tops should be scrubbed. The backs of front teeth can be cleaned with the toothbrush pointing into the mouth as in Figure 17.3. Some people find that method easier than using the brush with a side-to-side motion with these teeth.

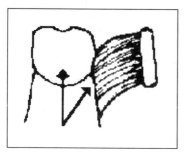

Figure 17.2

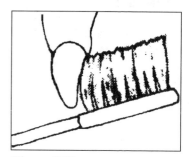

Figure 17.3

The skill of cleaning teeth efficiently is obviously best learnt in childhood, although reasonable efficiency is not likely to be achievable until somewhere between the ages of 4 and 7. On the other hand, in order to form good habits, babies should be encouraged to 'clean' their teeth as soon as they can hold a toothbrush, though they will need help from an adult until they can learn and habitually use a fully efficient method. People with dentures and orthodontic appliances need to be especially careful, because the denture or appliance often forms another natural trap for plaque and debris. All dentures should be cleaned on a regular, at least daily, basis. Anybody with dentures or orthodontic appliances should ask their dentist for advice (in a written form if possible) on how to care for both the denture/appliance and affected natural teeth. The care required can vary considerably between individuals and the nature of the fitting.

It may be helpful to conclude this section on day-to-day home care with brief comments about some of the other products marketed for home dental care. Electric tooth brushes are especially helpful for people who find it difficult to manipulate an ordinary toothbrush, maybe because they have arthritis in their hands for example. Some people prefer electric toothbrushes because they do an efficient job more quickly. It is possible to buy wooden toothpicks which have flat triangular ends rather than the rounded ends of cocktail sticks. If these toothpicks are used methodically by working round the mouth to treat each space between teeth then this process can be helpful. The toothpick should be inserted at an angle so that it works on the gum as well as the tooth. The gums are remarkably tough and benefit from such massage; if they bleed a little that does not matter and should not stop you using the toothpick. Any excessive bleeding or pain might be an indication of gum disease and could be a sign that a visit to the dentist would be sensible. Dental floss performs a similar function to toothpicks and also helps to remove plaque from the faces of teeth that are adjacent to other teeth. The basic way to use floss is to cut a length of about 1 foot or 30 cms. and wrap the ends round the fore fingers of each hand; then with one of those fingers in the mouth to gently engage the floss in the spaces between teeth and then to 'polish' the side surface of each of the teeth by a 'to and fro' and 'up and down' motion of the floss. Flossing is not easy to do properly and is time-consuming. It may be something to do once or twice a week rather than every day. Other devices are sold for cleaning the gaps between teeth. Two examples are toothbrushes with very small heads and electric high-pressure water jets.

The purpose of plaque disclosers is to show up the plaque which is otherwise transparent. To use a plaque discloser you rinse your teeth with the discloser and this then shows up the plaque by impregnating it with a colour. Some people like to use a plaque discloser before and after each occasion they clean their teeth. Plaque disclosers would certainly be useful as an aid to making sure a teeth cleaning technique is efficient. Mouth washes can be an additional aid for reducing plaque and helping healing after treatment for gum disease etc. They need to be used with care following the instructions on the container. Mouth washes are certainly not an alternative to using a toothbrush. It cannot be emphasised too often that cutting down on sugar intakes, plus regular and efficient cleaning of teeth, are the main day-to-day actions that everyone should take in order to reduce problems with teeth and gums.

Working with your dentist

The title and the major theme of this book are about dental patients working with their dentists. However, it is still probably useful to re-emphasise the importance of using dental services as an integral part of self-help in order to keep in good dental health. Apart from treatment when there are specific problems there are three aspects of working with your dentist that can help to ensure your continuing good dental health and that you obtain good value for money.

The first aspect is to ask for advice and instruction on preventive care. This is especially important for children. Instructions from a professional on teeth care can sometimes make more of an impact on children than the day-to-day comments of parents. Remember that most dentists would rather prevent dental problems than treat them. If you are registered with your dentist under an insurance scheme like Denplan etc, prevention is also very cost effective for the dentist.

The second aspect is that, however well you clean and otherwise look after your teeth and gums at home, there will almost certainly be some build-up of plaque and tartar in particular places on your teeth. This build-up is associated with the statistic that at any one time 80% of the adult population has gum disease at some level. A regular scale and polish will deal with this build up and again your dentist will be pleased to undertake this minor treatment on a regular six-month basis. The treatment only takes about ten minutes and can easily be built into an examination appointment.

The third aspect is your contribution to building up a good working relationship with your dentist. The comments here are largely common sense and good manners, but it may be worth reminding readers of some details, especially as many people find it difficult to overcome their near terror when conducting their business with their dentist and especially when visiting and talking to him or her. Points to remember are: (1) to keep appointments, or give as much notice as possible if there is a problem; (2) not to make unreasonable demands like asking for an emergency visit on a Sunday when you could cope until the Monday; (3) not to eat or drink strong-flavoured substances like garlic or beer before a dental appointment; (4) to try to be clear about symptoms. Writing them down may be helpful; the more you can contribute to your diagnosis and treatment, the more the dentist will be able to help (enlarging your knowledge of problems and treatments is of course the main purpose of this book); (5) to try to smile, say 'thank you', use the names of the dentist and assistant, and show that you feel involved in the smooth working of the practice.

Dental first aid

The purpose of this section is to provide information that can help families to make decisions about what they can do and what they should not do in the way of giving dental first aid.

In general the message about dental first aid is to keep it to an absolute minimum. There are two main instances when dental first aid might be necessary as follows: (1) if there is an accident that needs immediate action for the eventual success of any possible treatment; or (2) there is some reason why making an emergency visit to the dentist is impractical. A tooth being completely disturbed from its socket is an example of (1), being away from home in a remote place or somewhere where the dental services may be suspect are examples of (2). The normal alternative procedure is to use a phone to try to make an emergency visit to your dentist as soon as possible. On Christmas day and other similar days the dentist you speak to may consider that your emergency does not warrant an immediate visit and will suggest remedial action you can take until you can be seen, which will usually be on the next day.

The list of possible items that could be in a dental first aid kit is given only for guidance. Looking at the list and the details of the twelve situations where dental first aid might be needed you can decide what you would like to have available at home. The list is not given in any particular order except that the last two items might be difficult to buy. If you feel that you would like to have them, you may have to ask your dentist. The list is as follows: small mirror, hand mirror (both for looking at the backs of teeth), pen light, cotton wool, cotton buds, dental floss, wooden toothpicks, tweezers, oil of cloves, tincture of iodine, plaque discloser, a mouth wash sold for treating injuries to gums, painkillers (aspirin etc), gauze, temporary filling material, glue for replacing crowns.

In the twelve possibilities where dental first aid may be needed the last four are concerned with major accidental damage only. Some of the others may arise because of minor accidents.

Pain in a tooth: Where the pain is intermittent and not severe. Such pain should not be ignored as it is probably caused by a contact of saliva etc with dentine. This pain is then usually a sign that the enamel crown of the tooth has been breached. It is better to have a small filling at an early stage of the invasion by caries than a much bigger filling later, so the sooner the dentist is seen the better. If the condition is left the pain will sometimes seem to go away because dentine can adapt to being open to the mouth. First aid possibilities are to take normal painkillers such as aspirin or paracetamol and to examine the tooth to see if a hole or crack can be seen. If there is a hole then it can be treated with a cotton bud soaked in oil of cloves.

Severe toothache: Where the pain is severe and persistent, there may also be gum swelling and a throbbing sensation. Such a situation should always be treated as a dental emergency. The sooner a dentist is seen, the more likely it is that the tooth can be saved. Taking normal pain killers is the only possibility here as a temporary method of alleviating the pain. These should be taken by swallowing not held against the tooth!

Filling lost or a piece of a tooth breaks away: Rather surprisingly this situation does not always cause pain. Under normal circumstances arrange to visit the dentist as soon as possible. If there is pain then pain killers can be used as above. If the hole is a big one then a plug of cotton wool soaked in oil of cloves can be used as a temporary filling. If you are in a remote spot and have come prepared with temporary filling material then you can use that.

Objects wedged between teeth: The important point to remember in this situation is that it is easy to damage the teeth, especially if the object is hard like a piece of bone. You need to be gentle and not exert too much force. The use of dental floss, or a toothpick or tweezers in appropriate ways is likely to do the trick. If you are not successful then arrange to see a dentist as soon as possible, if the object is sharp then cover it with a piece of gauze in order to stop any damage to the mouth surfaces.

After an extraction the socket starts to bleed: For the background and more details of this condition refer to Chapter 11. The basic first aid for this problem is to apply pressure to the socket. The easiest way of applying such pressure is to bite on a folded piece of gauze. The gauze should be big enough to protrude well above the teeth on either side of the socket, so that the opposing tooth can exert the pressure. The pressure should be exerted for five minutes at a time until the bleeding stops. If no success is achieved then treat it as a medical emergency.

A crown or a bridge becomes detached: This problem is quite common and is normally easy to remedy. If the detached crown or bridge is taken to the dentist it can usually be replaced without any problem. The main thing for the patient to do is to retrieve the crown or bridge. If it has become very loose and an immediate emergency visit to a dentist is not possible then it should be detached very carefully from its supporting structures. If the crown or bridge is swallowed then it would still be best to retrieve it if you can deal with the mess etc! DIY refixing of a bridge or crown should not normally be attempted. The only possible exception to this rule is if such an eventuality has been allowed for when help from a suitably qualified dentist is a week or more away. Even in this case the special crown fixing glue must be used, otherwise the tooth might be badly damaged or the person poisoned.

Fixed orthodontic appliance becomes detached: These appliances are often complex structures with several wires and different types of attachments to teeth. They should be monitored carefully on a daily basis and any problems should be dealt with by the dentist as an emergency. In this case no DIY is ever possible and first aid should consist of protecting the mouth by covering any sharp ends of wire etc with gauze.

Removable orthodontic appliance or a denture breaks or becomes loose:
The main point to establish for these situations is that no attempt should be
made to keep the appliance or denture in place. The denture or appliance
should not be placed in the mouth until it has been repaired. A repair and
refitting by the dentist should normally be arranged as soon as possible,
although dentures can sometimes be repaired in a specialist dental workshop.
The only possible exception to a repair by a dental professional is if you have
prepared for such an eventuality when help from somebody suitably qualified
is a week or more away. Even in this case the special glue must be used,
otherwise the denture might be badly damaged or the person poisoned.

The four possibilities concerned with serious accidental damage

Whenever there is an accident that creates any possibility of damage to teeth
and gums then an appointment should be made to see the dentist. Such a visit
should be made even if there is no pain and no visible sign of damage. Chapter
14 on accidental damage gives the background details that explain why such
visits are urgent and important.

Injured tongue or lip: Apply pressure to the bleeding area with a clean
handkerchief or other cloth. If a swelling is present apply cold compresses. If
bleeding does not stop or if there is much damage to the soft tissues then go to
the nearest hospital casualty department.

Loosened or broken tooth: Gently clean the injured area with warm water.
Cold compresses applied to the face may help minimise swelling. Go to the
dentist immediately and take the broken fragment of tooth. If the broken
fragment cannot be found it may be necessary for the dentist to refer you to the
nearest hospital casualty department for a chest X-ray to be taken.

Tooth knocked out: If the tooth is a permanent tooth then there is a good
chance that it can be successfully replanted in its socket. To be successful this
operation has to be done more or less immediately, so it may well be necessary
to do it yourself. The tooth should only be handled by touching the crown. If
the tooth is quite clean then leave it alone but if it has been badly contaminated
with any dirt, then wash it gently with warm, slightly salted, tap water or milk.
Do not scrub or apply any form of antiseptic or disinfectant. If you are prepared
to replace the tooth yourself, then push the tooth gently back into its socket,
still holding it by the crown only. If this is done quickly it is not usually painful.
Next, the patient should bite on a solidly folded cloth, handkerchief or piece of
gauze in order to hold the tooth in place, this should be kept in place for at least
one hour. A dentist should still be seen as soon as possible as the tooth will

probably need to be splinted. As an alternative a dentist should be seen within half an hour of the accident occurring. The tooth should be taken to the dentist stored against the cheek in the patient's mouth or in milk. If the accident happened outside surgery hours then contact the nearest hospital emergency department for information about emergency dental services. Baby teeth that are completely knocked out are not usually replanted, but the dentist or local casualty department should normally still be consulted as an emergency.

Possible jaw fracture: If possible, keep the jaws fixed in a closed position by using some form of tie such as a scarf, towel or bandage wrapped around the top of the head and under the jaw firmly but gently. Make sure that there is no blood at the back of the mouth to cause choking and be prepared to release the bandage quickly if the patient starts to vomit. Applying cool compresses will minimise swelling. This is a very serious injury so you should dial 999 or go immediately to the nearest hospital casualty department.

Other sources of information

There are several bodies and authorities who will supply information about health and dentistry in particular. It is possible that some readers will need 'hard' information occasionally. Examples are choosing or complaining about a dentist, or wanting help with a particular problem like an elderly parent refusing to go to see a dentist. There may be other occasions when non-urgent personal advice and help could be useful. One example of less 'hard' information could be finding help to overcome the terror at the idea of visiting a dentist which some sources say is experienced by some 20% of the population. At the other end of the information scale, teachers and librarians, and parents whose children are studying or doing a project on dental matters, will often like to obtain 'soft' information about dental matters: leaflets, booklets etc. which can be used to expand knowledge about teeth, gums and their care.

Finding information that might help with the choice of dentists is dealt with in detail in Chapter 18. There are likely to be some readers who want to follow up complaints so that issue is dealt with next. Anybody unhappy with some aspect of their dental treatment should first make every effort to discuss the matter with their dentist. For NHS patients the next formal stage is to complain in writing to their local Family Health Service Authority (FHSA), or in Scotland to the Health Board, and in Northern Ireland to the Health and Social Services Board. There is a time limit for a formal written complaint to be made. It is obviously best to phone first using numbers as found under '(county name) Health Authority' in local phone directories. Your local Community Health Council may also be able to help, and again the number will be in your local phone book under '(county name) Community Health Council'. If unhappy with the way this level of complaint is dealt with then the next stage is to complain to the appropriate Health Service Commissioner as given below. Complaints about private treatment can be addressed to an insurer if there is one, otherwise the only avenue for complaint is the General Dental Council, though you should be warned that they only deal with cases of serious professional misconduct.

Health Service Commissioner Addresses:-

England – Church House, Great Smith Street, London, SW1P 3BW, 0171 276 2035
Scotland – 2nd Floor, 11 Melville Crescent, Edinburgh, EH3 7LU, 0131 225 7465
Wales – 4th Floor Pearl Assurance House, Greyfriars Road, Cardiff, CF1 3AG, 01222 394621
Northern Ireland – The Ombudsman, Freepost, Belfast, BT1 6BR, 0800 282036

The other contact points given in this chapter include brief notes on what they will provide.
   Very often when somebody has concerns it can be helpful to discuss matters with somebody on the phone in the first instance. There is a free phone number that might provide help for dental matters:-

0800 665544 is the free phone number of a service provided by the NHS to give detailed help to the public. If you use this number you will be routed through to an advisory service for your local health authority, they will give advice on all NHS matters, including advice on personal problems. This service is available Monday to Friday 9.30 am – 5.00 pm.

For the general public, the General Dental Council is not just the final court for making complaints. In particular there is a separate section which is a charitable trust whose purpose is partly to provide information on dental matters. They will send literature to inform about dental matters, including leaflets produced especially for children and material about jobs associated with dentistry. They are very helpful and it is well worth contacting them:-
The General Dental Council, 37 Wimpole Street, London, W1M 8DQ, 0171 486 2171

The British Dental Association is a body that supplies information and services to dentists who pay an annual fee to join. They do, however, provide a useful general service to the public which is the possibility of talking to a dentist on the phone at some time during the day from Monday to Friday. This service may be of use in order to provide information on problem cases or special circumstances. The British Dental Association does not send out literature to the general public.

The British Dental Association, 64 Wimpole Street, London, W1M 8AL, 0171 935 0875

The British Dental Health Foundation is a privately funded charity one of whose purposes is to provide information and help on dental matters to the general public. One distinctive offering they make is a helpline for people who are worried about visiting a dentist. They are also a good source of literature and general information.

The British Dental Health Foundation, Eastlands Court, St Peter's Road, Rugby, Warwickshire, CV21 3QP, 01788 546365

The Health Education Authority is a national government-funded body set up to provide information on health matters to the general public. They fund and initiate the production of literature on health matters, which includes dentistry. They will send out useful information in various forms.

The Health Education Authority, Hamilton House, Mabledon Place, London, WC1H 9TX, 0171 383 3833

For teachers, librarians and parents the best source of general information is likely to be local. For dentistry the best source could well be associated with the school's dental service. The main purpose of this service is to provide a regular check on the dental state of every child in a state school. Parents will receive notification of the fact their children have been inspected on three or four occasions during their compulsory time at school. Another function of this service is to provide dental education in schools. As a part of this education provision there is likely to be a central store of literature, learning aids etc. which can be of great help to teachers, librarians and parents. There may also be a very limited number of staff who will visit schools to provide a special learning session. The official name for the section which provides this service is 'Community Dental Services' and the phone number should be listed under the local Health Trust. From experience of looking at phone books for various areas, finding this number in the phone book is not always easy. It is probably best to look under 'Health', phone the main number listed and explain your needs to them. There is also likely to be other local provision for providing health information, maybe 'Health Information' shops or other similar projects. These may be listed in the phone book under 'Health' or under '(county name) Health Authority'.

Chapter 18

Choosing a Dentist

the NHS, private care, insurance schemes

Introduction

The purpose of this chapter is to give readers information about choices when changing dentists or when circumstances mean that a switch to private dental care is a possibility.

It is sensible to think through and discuss requirements when considering the choice of a particular dentist or dental practice; suggestions for factors to consider are given next in this chapter under the heading of **Choosing a dentist**. A major choice available is whether to register a family as NHS or private patients. This choice will certainly depend on financial circumstances and it may also depend on where you live as NHS dentists are very rare in some areas. Detailed descriptions of the differences between NHS registration and private registration, including financial considerations, are given in this chapter under the headings **Registering with a dentist under the NHS scheme, and Registering as a private patient.** The decision to register as a private patient may well be associated with joining an insurance scheme. There are two basically different ways of insuring for private dental care. For the first of these patients pay a fixed sum each month to the insurer who then pays the dentist to carry out a limited selection of treatments for no further charge (except for dental laboratory charges). Details of four suppliers of this type of dental insurance are given under the heading of **Capitation schemes**. The second type of dental insurance scheme involves the patient paying the dentist and then claiming all or part of the cost back from the insurer. Details of four suppliers of this type of dental insurance are given under the heading of **Insurance schemes.**

Choosing a dentist

The choice of a dentist is an important decision. Any person or a family needs to feel confident about the nature of the advice and treatments they receive, and comfortable about arranging appointments and undertaking visits. Going to the dentist is rarely likely to be a pleasurable experience, but if you are relatively relaxed this can be a great help in achieving full co-operation with your dentist and the corresponding effectiveness of the treatment. One aspect of the choice should not be a major worry because the great majority of dentists are concerned professionals. There are extremely few dentists who are incompetent or deliberately slapdash in order to make more money. On the other hand dentists are human. They do make mistakes, they can respond to pressures of time, money and their own health and they can also react to the actions and attitudes of their patients. It is certainly likely that there are some dentists in your area who would suit your requirements better than others.

It is sensible to think through your requirements and to consider all the factors that might affect your choice of a dentist or dental practice. You do need to make sure you know what you want! One way of considering your requirements is to establish criteria for comparing dentists or dental practices. The criteria could include:-

1. The size of the practice, the number of dentists, other dental staff and receptionists.

2. The situation of the practice, how far it is from home work and school, what parking is available at or near the surgery, public transport connection times, access and facilities for any disabled members of the family.

3. What emergency arrangements are available for weekends etc.

4. Is the practice sympathetic to children? Is the sex of your dentist an issue?

5. The way the dentists in the practice work: are they prepared to discuss the details of treatments and take time over decision-making and treatment? Are they careful to keep pain to a minimum and waiting times not too long. Are they prepared to refer some treatments to other dentists or specialists?

6. What are the registration possibilities and costs? NHS for all, or NHS just for children, or NHS for all that qualify for full free treatment and no others? If private registration is offered then what are the costs for standard treatments, how are these costs estimated and what insurance schemes are supported?

7. The range of treatments on offer; it is possible that some practices may not offer treatments such as orthodontics, endodontics or complex bridge work.

8. The age(s) and qualifications of the dentist(s).
Along with deciding on the criteria you should also obtain information on local choices. Some possibilities are:-

Yellow pages

These will list all dentists who have registered their phone number as a business number with BT. From yellow pages you can see the size of practice, which might range from one dentist to five dentists (rarely more than five). Possible advantages and drawbacks of small and large practices are:

Smaller practices: Advantages: Likely to be more personal – a 'family' practice. Drawbacks: Fewer expensive resources, greater need to refer and the backup for the dentist being ill or on holiday comes from outside the practice.

Larger practices: Advantages: More resources and range of backup facilities and expertise and a rota usually operates for emergency treatment. Drawbacks: Could be less personal, though patients usually stick to one dentist in the group.

Ask others

Choose people with similar needs e.g. children or an age group and discuss the criteria above. If people say a dentist never hurts this is not the only important factor!

Contact regional offices of

Family Health Service Authority (FHSA) in England
Health Board in Scotland
Health and Social Services Board in Northern Ireland
Numbers for these are in the phone book.

These bodies keep lists of all dentists in their area and whether they take NHS patients or not. They should be able to give names for 5 or 6 practices in any area that fulfil particular criteria, in particular their position about accepting patients under the NHS scheme. Many thousands of people each year use this service.

Obtain practice leaflets if available

Practices should produce a leaflet which includes names, sex and date of qualification of all the dentists, opening hours, access details (wheelchairs etc), other staff like dental hygienists employed and any specialisations of the dentists in the practice.

Note: Don't always pick the nearest dentist, and be prepared to change if you are not happy with the services you receive. Changing a dentist is simple. It needs a registration with a new dentist and informing the previous dentist. Remember using a dentist or dental practice is a two-way relationship. The most vital part of this co-operation is that you should keep appointments on time and give the best notice possible if there is a problem about keeping an appointment. Other points about responsibilities when using dentist and other dental services are given under personal dental care in Chapter 17.

Registering with a dentist under the NHS scheme

The regulations under which payments are made to dentists under the NHS scheme are rather complex. It is useful for prospective patients to have some idea of how the scheme works in order to achieve the best option, both in terms of money and treatment, for a given set of circumstances for an individual or a family. Under the NHS scheme dentists are paid a fixed amount each month for each person under the age of 18 on their list and are expected to provide any treatment necessary from that payment. Having under 18s registered therefore provides a regular steady income for the dentist. This method of payment also provides an inducement for the dentist to promote preventive measures for under 18s, as such measures are likely to decrease the amount of time-consuming treatments, like fillings, that have to be given.

For each adult that is registered with a dentist under the NHS scheme the dentist receives a small fixed amount each year. These annual payments also provide a limited regular income. The main income from adults registered under the NHS scheme is based on payment for treatments, so the more treatments a dentist does in a week the more money he/she receives. Under the NHS scheme all treatments are itemised and the dentist is paid a fixed sum of money for a particular treatment. Unless the patient qualifies for free treatment, the patient pays 80% of the fixed sum and the NHS pays 20%. From the point of view of an adult who has to pay the 80% it is probably not the fact that the NHS pays the 20% that is important, but the fact that the payment is fixed. By contrast a dentist treating somebody privately has the freedom to set their own charges which are normally about one and a half times the NHS figure, but can also be three or more times the NHS figure.

NHS treatment is free for under 18s, under 19s in full time education, pregnant women or women who have had a baby in the last twelve months, anyone receiving Income Support or Family Credit. People receiving a disability allowance may also qualify for free treatment and should check with the DSS. For each of these groups the NHS pays the full 100% of the fixed charge for treatments given. Others on low incomes may be able to obtain some help for payment for dental treatment in the form of an additional proportion of the cost of treatment. They should fill in form AB11 obtainable from the DSS or their GP. All others registered under the NHS scheme have to pay the full 80% of the cost of examination and treatment.

The NHS system is designed to give dentists a reasonable income for a sensible number of patients and treatments. Like any other nationally imposed system it is not perfect. Some dentists will want to generate higher incomes than others and some dentists will have higher overheads than others. Because dentists are paid largely by the number of treatments they do, all NHS treatment will be subject to time pressures. The NHS arrangements for dental treatment are more complex than treatment from a doctor because most patients have to pay a proportion of the costs of all dental treatment, whereas medical treatment is free apart from prescription charges.

The prices charged for NHS treatment are fixed nationally. Dentists have to keep a record of all work done and are paid by charging patients immediately after a course of treatment and by submitting the details of all treatments to the relevant NHS body. The fact that NHS charges are fixed nationally also affects the regional variation in the numbers of dentists who offer NHS treatments. A dentist who lives in an area with high overheads in terms of property values, staff wages etc. might find it more difficult to achieve a good income from NHS treatments than a dentist who works in a lower overhead region. One consequence is a North-South divide in the easy availability of NHS dental treatment.

Dentists are also free to take only certain categories of NHS patients. They may for example only take those whose treatment is free under the NHS. In order to illustrate the effect of the freedom of dentists to choose which categories of patients they will treat under the NHS, the national figures show that about 50% of dentists will accept all adults under NHS arrangements, an additional 30% will accept patients who qualify for free treatment under NHS but will not accept adults who have to pay for some of their treatment. It follows that around 20% of dentists offer only private treatment. Dentists are also free to inform their present patients that they will no longer accept them under the NHS scheme. Some 800,000 patients were deregistered from the NHS scheme in this way in the years 1993 and 1994. The lack of dentists who offer NHS treatment in some areas can cause a major difficulty for those who are relatively poor, but who do not qualify for state benefits. Many people with their own homes but whose only income is the state old age pension are one example.

Some treatments or materials are not available under the NHS scheme, but patients can choose to have a mix of NHS and private treatment if they do not want to accept such limitations. Details of where such situations can occur are given in the main sections describing treatments in the book, but some examples are given here in order to illustrate this point. Even if you are registered as an NHS patient, most NHS dentists will offer or suggest payment for treatment under certain conditions. One example is the use of white composite filling on back teeth if the patient wants to choose this option (see Chapter 9); another example is the possibility of an expensive bridge rather than a cheaper partial denture (see Chapter 11). It should be noted that in these cases the treatments are either all NHS or all private, so in the first example for the white composite option, it is not possible to charge the preparation to the NHS and the filling material privately. It may well also happen that patients registered under the NHS may be advised by their NHS dentist to visit a private specialist for particular treatments not available under the NHS, such as orthodontics for cosmetic reasons or in order have implants. Readers should be prepared to discuss costs and methods of payment along with the nature and effects of treatments even if they are registered as NHS patients.

Registering as a private patient

As there are a growing number of dental practices which no longer take patients under the NHS scheme, registering with one of these practices is the next option to be considered. Generally speaking dentists who offer only private treatment allow more time to discuss treatments with patients and more time for the actual treatments. This is probably the major difference from the patient's point of view between NHS and private treatment.

If patients opt for private treatment then there are basically four different ways in which the costs can be met. The first way is to pay for each individual treatment as it is needed. The second way is to be employed by a business that covers the cost of dental services for its employees. The third way is to join a 'capitation' scheme run by a national company, or an individual dental practice, or a group of dental practices. Capitation schemes operate by the patient paying a fixed amount per month for which a range of basic treatments like fillings are covered without further payments. The fourth option is to join an 'insurance' scheme. If a patient uses an insurance scheme then they pay a fixed amount each month to the insurer and claim for treatments from the insurer.

The costs of private treatment for patients, if they are not in a capitation scheme, are based on individual treatments. The charge for a treatment will include elements for direct costs like the dentist's time, materials, use of X-rays as well as indirect costs like rent, phone bills etc. Patients will not generally receive itemised accounts. The dentist will give them an overall estimate for the cost of a course of treatment and the final bill will be for a single global sum. The main benefit of using capitation or insurance schemes for the patient is that a significant part of the costs of normal treatment can be spread out rather than needing expensive one-off payments. A benefit for the dentist registering with a capitation scheme is that it cuts down the paper work to some extent, while also providing a steady income. Another benefit for dentists is that they are likely to have fewer unpaid bills to deal with. Private dental practices must be seen as commercial enterprises. Many such practices will want some guarantee of payment, such as taking an imprint of a credit card, before beginning treatment.

For those that can afford the costs, either directly or through a capitation or an insurance scheme, then they might well wish to opt for the dentist to allocate more time to examination, discussion and treatment. Other differences for private treatments will be the availability of wider options in materials, equipment and treatments. Expensive bridges and implants are not available as NHS treatments and as these treatments can cost several thousand pounds this is not surprising. Case studies 6,8,10 and 11 in Chapter 5 illustrate how this wider range of choices can be very important to individuals in particular circumstances. Private dental practices are also likely to be more lavishly furnished and staffed.

If dental patients decide to switch from NHS registration to private registration then it is likely that using a capitation or insurance scheme will be beneficial. There are two main reasons why people are likely to benefit from using a nationally based capitation or insurance scheme. The first benefit is financial in that for a fixed regular sum it is likely that the most common dental treatments such as fillings and extractions will be covered without any further additional payment, although there can be considerable reservations to this blanket coverage as described in detail for each scheme. The second benefit of belonging to a nationally based scheme rather than a local scheme, or paying for each individual treatment, is that there is an immediate and relatively low level point of referral if there are any worries about the quality or nature of treatments received or if you want to change dentists.

A major difference between capitation and insurance schemes is that it is a dental practice that registers with a capitation scheme. Patients using that dental practice then have either to pay for individual treatments or belong to the particular capitation scheme chosen by the practice. By contrast it is the patient who chooses the insurance scheme. They can then use any dentist and claim the cost of treatment from the insurance scheme.

By far the most common form of dental insurance is through capitation schemes. To make sure that you obtain the best value for money from using a capitation scheme you need to appreciate the way these schemes work from the point of view of not only patients, but also dentists, and the scheme providers. It may also be useful to contrast dental schemes to medical schemes because the two normally fulfil entirely different functions within the national picture. In general, medical schemes are an insurance for treatment beyond the primary care which is the first point of contact for patients. In other words medical insurance schemes do not pay GPs, they only pay for treatment in hospitals and by specialists. By contrast the normal dental capitation scheme pays for primary care and not for any specialist or hospital treatment.

Capitation Schemes

In order to appreciate the way that capitation schemes work, it may be easiest to start from the point of view of the dentist. Under a capitation scheme the dentist will be paid a fixed amount each month for each patient registered. For this amount the dentist has to supply a specified range of treatments without any additional charges. It follows that from the dentist's point of view the monthly payment needs to be related in some way to the number of relevant treatments patients are likely to require. Ways of dealing with this factor include: (a) screening patients before they are accepted under a scheme; (b) having different rates for different patients; (c) excluding some treatments either for all patients or particular patients under a time limit or a screening process. In fact there is usually a mix of all three of these processes. The different schemes have different ways of dealing with this necessity of limiting the dentist's workload as will be explained for each scheme. Dental patients registered with a scheme pay their contributions to the scheme provider, not to the dentist. In general the scheme providers make money by taking a small percentage of the amounts that members of the scheme pay. Scheme providers may also charge dentists for using the scheme, but as all dentists within a scheme are checked for quality control that charge has some benefits for patients.

There are three general points on the nature of capitation schemes. The first point is that in order to use a scheme you have to use a dentist who is registered with the scheme. The most likely reason for patients to opt for a particular capitation scheme is that their present dental practice, or a dental practice they choose when moving to a new area, is registered with that scheme. The dental practice will then require all patients to either pay for individual treatments or register with the chosen scheme. It is also possible that you may prefer a particular scheme, in which case phoning the scheme provider will provide a list of dentists registered with that scheme in the area. At present very few dentists are registered with more than one scheme, so choices for dental patients can be limited. The second point is that the amount you pay per month to a capitation scheme is largely decided by your dentist, so it is well worth discussing the reasons why you are in a particular payment band and re-negotiating the amount you pay if you think it is too much after a period of time. The third point is that all four schemes have the common features of covering for emergency treatment abroad with an English speaking dentist if possible, and for providing advice and treatment for preventative care.

The details concerning four capitation schemes are given by listing the schemes in alphabetical order: BUPA, CDC, Denplan, Norwich Union.

BUPA DentalCover

BUPA DentalCover was launched in October 1993 and in 1996 had around 60,000 subscribers. The amount paid per month is on a variable scale depending on an initial assessment by the dentist and the range of treatments to be covered. The standard range of treatments covered normally includes the basic range of those that commonly concern most of the population and in general are the treatments covered in Chapters 9 to 12 in this book. This range normally includes major restorative work like crowns, bridges and dentures. The monthly subscription and what is to be covered are set by your dentist. The subscription is normally between £6 and £30 per month with most people paying somewhere in the range £11 – £13 per month. Patients should be re-assessed each year and should be aware of this fact and be prepared to negotiate. They should also be quite clear about what is covered and not covered in their case. The details given in this book will be especially helpful for such discussions and negotiations.

Not covered under BUPA DentalCover are: dental laboratory charges for crowns, bridges and dentures; treatments classified as cosmetic, which include orthodontic treatment as in Chapter 13, so a teenager needing treatment for misaligned teeth is likely to prove expensive; in general specialist treatments as described in Chapter 15 are not covered. This will include implants and dental surgery.

Contact address: BUPA DentalCover, Heron House, 8-10 Christchurch Road, Bournemouth, BH1 3NP,
Phone: 0800 230 230

CDC Cost Care

CDC Cost Care has fewer subscribers than the other three capitation plans. The amount paid per month is on a variable scale depending on the nature and position of the dental practice. The flyer for CDC says that the average amount paid per week is the price of a packet of cigarettes, so the cost per month is probably in the range of £8 – £12. Patients have to be examined and passed as dentally fit before they can join the scheme. The range of treatments covered is fixed and includes the basic range of those that commonly concern most of the population and are the treatments covered in Chapters 9 to 12 in this book. This range normally includes major restorative work like crowns, bridges and dentures.

CDC Cost Care are very explicit about what is not covered as follows: the services of a dental technician, i.e. charges for crowns, bridges and dentures; referral to a consultant; treatments classified as cosmetic, which includes orthodontic treatment as in Chapter 13, so a teenager's treatment for misaligned teeth is likely to prove expensive; in general the specialist treatments as described in Chapter 15 are not covered. This will include implants and dental surgery; some drug prescriptions; treatment after surgery hours. The other exclusion under CDC is interesting because it is a default for visiting the dentist less than once a year. If the dentist judges that damage is a result of such neglect then the treatment will not be covered.

Contact address:
CDC, Westbourne House, 115 Station Road, Hayes, Middlesex, UB3 4BX
Phone: 0181 848 1028

Denplan

Denplan is the oldest dental capitation scheme and with over 500,000 subscribers in 1996 is also the largest plan in the UK. Denplan was started by a group of dentists but was taken over by the medical insurer PPP (Private Patients Plan) in 1995. When joining the scheme patients are assessed by the dentist and placed in one of five payment bands. A person in their twenties with healthy teeth is likely to be in a cheaper band than someone in their fifties with a poor dental history and a mouthful of fillings. The size of payments for each band also depends on the location of the practice.

Under the Denplan scheme all patients in every one of the five bands are covered for the same range of treatments and also have to pay individually for the same exclusions.

Treatments covered under Denplan are basically the range of those that commonly concern most of the population and in general are the treatments covered in Chapters 9 to 12 in this book. This means that routine examinations, fillings, extractions and replacement with bridges and dentures, root canal fillings and crowns, and non surgical treatment of gum problems are all covered under Denplan.

Not covered under Denplan are: the dental laboratory charges for crowns, bridges and dentures; treatments classified as cosmetic, which includes orthodontic treatment as in Chapter 13, so a teenager's treatment for misaligned teeth is likely to prove expensive; in general the specialist treatments as described in Chapter 15 are not covered. This will include implants and dental surgery. Accidental damage is not covered under the general scheme but can be allowed for with supplementary insurance cover.

Denplan labels the five bands as A,B,C,D and E. In 1995 the monthly payments for Band A were apx. £6.50, and for Band E apx. £21. The most common payment for Denplan in 1995 was around £10 per month. Under Denplan it is the dentist that sets the rate for each band and also the dentist who decides the band under which a particular patient will join the scheme. It follows that when people join the Denplan scheme some negotiation on costs with the dentist may be a possibility. Factors like discounts for families etc. might also be negotiable.

Contact address:
Denplan Ltd., Denplan Court, Victoria Road, Winchester, SO23 7RG
Phone: 01962 866662, Fax:- 01963 840846

Norwich Union Healthcare

This dental capitation scheme started in 1992. Norwich Union cannot give the number of people who subscribe to the dental scheme as such people often have medical insurance as well, but the figures are likely to be similar to BUPA at around 60,000 in 1996. When patients join the Norwich scheme they are placed in one of three 'plans'. Each of these plans requires a different monthly payment, but each plan also includes a different range of treatments. The plans are labelled Plan I, Plan II and Plan III. Plan III includes most of the normally required treatments people encounter in as in Chapters 9 to 12 in this book. These treatments include fillings, root canal fillings and crowns, non-surgical treatment of gum disease, extractions but not bridges or dentures. All patients in a Norwich practice will pay the same rate for Plan III in 1995 this rate was around £9 per month. The great majority of patients registered under the Norwich scheme are placed in Plan III. The reason for having the other two plans is to provide flexibility for the dentist when registering new patients for the scheme. If the dentist used the Norwich scheme as their main method of payment and it was only Plan III that was available then they would have to refuse to register some new patients because their dental condition was unsatisfactory and the amount paid per month would nowhere near cover the treatment that would have to be provided. It follows that plans I and II cover smaller ranges of treatments. Plan II covers fillings and extractions but not root canal fillings or crowns, and Plan I does not even cover fillings and extractions. The list of items covered for Plan I is: examinations and consultations, X-rays, dental health instruction, fluoride treatments, scale and polish, worldwide emergency cover. The other two plans also include these. The charges for Plans I and II are set low. In 1995 they were about £4.50 and £5.50 per month.

Not covered under any of the Norwich Plans are: 40 % of the cost of treatment if there are dental laboratory charges for crowns; treatments classified as cosmetic, which includes orthodontic treatment as in Chapter 13, so a teenager's treatment for misaligned teeth is likely to prove expensive; bridges and dentures; in general the specialist treatments as described in Chapter 15 are not covered, this will include implants and dental surgery; accidental damage is also not covered.

While the charges for each plan are fixed nationally it is the dentist who decides which plan a new patient may join, so patients registering under the Norwich scheme should be prepared to discuss the details of the plan options before they agree to register.

Contact address: Dental Care, Norwich Union Healthcare, FREEPOST, KE8493, London, EC3B 3DP
Phone: 0800 515876

Insurance Schemes

The four insurance schemes dealt with in this section offer very different facilities to each other at very different costs. The main features they have in common are: (1) that there is no restriction on choice of dentist; (2) unlike capitation schemes they cover accidental damage and referral to a consultant; (3) the dental cover can be, and normally is, a part of an overall medical package. Another big difference from the patient point of view when using an insurance scheme rather than a capitation scheme is that the patient has to deal with the paperwork, by filling in claim forms, obtaining dentist signatures etc.

The details of the four insurance schemes are given in alphabetical order:-
Clinicare, HSA, Prime Health, Western Provident.

Clinicare

Clinicare provides dental cover as a feature of the option plan entitled 'Carte Blanche'. Under this plan patients are covered for just about any medical, dental or optical treatment, including treatment by GPs. The dental cover has virtually no exclusions, but there are price limits: £40 per filling and £300 per set of dentures for example. As can be imagined such overall cover is not cheap. There are three price bands A, B and C depending on the type of hospitals that can be available and the age of the patient. To give an indication of prices in 1995, a single person in the age range 40-44, choosing band C, would pay around £53 per month for 'Carte Blanche', at age 70+ this rises to £96 per month. 'Carte Blanche' is the sort of cover that is sometimes provided for busy executives as a part of an overall remuneration package.

Contact address: Strasbourgeoise UK, Private Health Insurance Services Ltd. 195 Knightsbridge, LONDON, SW7 1RE
Phone: 0171 589 8755

HSA

HSA stands for the Hospital Saving Association. It is a non-profit-making Benevolent Association. The way it works is that there are four bands of weekly payments per family. These payments range from £1.10 per week to £6.60 per week per family. The benefits are based on paying half the bill for each member of the family when they require treatments that need payment. The 'half' is subject to a cash limit, so for dental treatment the yearly cash limit per person is £22 in Band 1 and £132 per person in Band 4. This cash payment can be for payments needed for NHS registered patients receiving non NHS treatments, for composite fillings rather than amalgam fillings on back teeth for example. HSA covers over two million people in the UK. It seems to offer good value for money, especially for large families. The patient has to deal with the paperwork. For dental treatment that will mean filling in a claim form and supplying an original dated receipt.

Contact address: HSA, Hambledon House, Andover, Hants, SP10 1LQ
Phone: 01264 353211
or: HSA, 28 Stafford Street, Edinburgh, EH3 7BD
Phone: 0131 226 4824

Prime Health

The provisions of this package are rather different as 'low level' treatment like inspections and fillings are not covered. Some of the treatments that do qualify for payments are root canal treatment, crowns, bridges and dentures. This dental insurance can only be used as an option by people who have medical insurance with Prime Health. In 1996 the cost of the dental option ranged from £3 per month for a single person to £7.50 a month for a family. The payments for treatment can be made even if the treatment was given under the NHS scheme and would then usually completely cover the cost of the treatment.

Contact address: Prime Health Limited, St Christopher House, Wellington Road South, Stockport, Cheshire, SK2 6YF
Phone: 01483 306171

Western Provident Association
WPA provide dental cover under a scheme known as PROVIdental. The payment for this scheme is fixed and is the same for everybody. In 1995 this was £6 per month or £63 per year. This scheme is basically very different from the other dental schemes. Its design is more like a typical medical scheme in that it mostly covers uncommon oral problems like cancer or dental injuries rather than day-to-day occurrences like fillings and dentures etc. Common treatments are covered but only to a very limited extent. Members of the scheme can claim a maximum of £10 per year for routine dental examination and £18 per year for preventive care and any dental treatment.

Contact address: Western Provident Association Ltd. Rivergate House, Blackbrook Park, Taunton, Somerset, TA1 2PE
Phone: 01823 623385

Chapter 19

Becoming a Dentist

or other dental professional

Introduction

The purpose of this chapter is to give brief descriptions of the careers that are associated with dental care and the qualifications needed to start on the training courses that qualify people for these careers. The details given in this chapter are only intended to provide information at a basic level, with the idea that it will provide some guidance to teenagers who may be thinking about possible careers. The details given are largely taken from a pack which is sent out free by the General Dental Council and anybody who has a particular interest should phone them and ask for a copy of this pack. The pack also contains a list of educational institutions and hospitals where qualifications for dental careers can be obtained. That information is not given in this chapter.

There are five main 'job descriptions' for possible careers in dental care with the titles: dental surgeon (or dentist), dental surgery assistant, dental technician, dental hygienist and dental therapist. There are about 40,000 dental surgeons in the UK and broadly speaking every dental surgeon will need a dental surgery assistant, so these two jobs need a fairly high annual input of people. There are about one third of this number of dental technicians. There are many fewer dental hygienists and dental therapists. Probably something like 3000 hygienists and 300 therapists in the UK. Both hygienists and therapists normally have to first qualify as dental surgery assistants and then take additional courses to obtain the necessary further qualifications.

Dental Surgeon (or Dentist)

You will already know a good deal about what a dentist does. This is a professional job with a professional rate of pay. In 1995 the pay for an experienced dentist was normally at least £40,000 per year. Dental surgeons are talented and special people. At the very least they have to be very good academically, have good eyesight and be manually dextrous, be able to be patient and understanding with people. Very often dentists are set up to work as a small business, in which case they also have to have good business sense and good man-management skills. While the majority of dentists are male, manual strength is not needed and the job is equally suitable for women. Being a dentist is often a very stressful occupation, mainly because many dental patients are worried and tense; such stress in the people dealt with on a daily basis is bound to affect the person responsible for administering the treatment.

The minimum time to qualify as a dentist is five years. These five years are spent at one of the fourteen universities in the UK that have 'dental schools'. Seven of these universities also offer a 'pre-dental year' for people who do not have relevant initial qualifications. They may have taken arts A levels rather than science A levels for example. In this case it will take six years to qualify. The normal first degree qualification for dentistry is a BDS (Bachelor of Dental Surgery). Each university will have their own entry requirements for students wishing to take BDS courses, but as a general guideline the minimum will include three A levels or equivalent, normally to be passed at one of the top two grades, and the subjects to include either biology or chemistry or both. While most people who qualify from a university as dental surgeons enter general practice, there are other avenues available such as hospital work, the schools service, the armed forces, industry and teaching. This second selection is generally salaried and pensionable employment rather than the payment for numbers of treatments and numbers of patients that is normal in general practice.

Dental Surgery Assistant

You will have a good idea of what is involved in this job, as every time you receive dental treatment a dental surgery assistant (DSA) will have called you in to the surgery, assisted the dentist with your treatment and dealt with administrative arrangements like sorting out payment and signing forms. In a practice which has just one dentist, the DSA will also act as the receptionist, arranging appointments etc. Larger practices generally employ receptionists separately. The pay for a young unqualified DSA can start from around £6,000 per year; an experienced and fully qualified DSA is likely to receive about £10,000 to £12,000 per year.

Dental surgery assistants can become qualified by obtaining the National Certificate for Dental Surgery Assistants. There are no academic entry requirements or age limits for people who want to enter the examinations and practical assessments that lead to achieving this qualification. There are short government training schemes which give a grounding in the different aspects of the job. Anybody who is at all interested in becoming a DSA would probably benefit by attending one of these courses. There are two basic routes to achieving the qualification: the first is to combine academic study with actual work in a dental practice. This will mean going to evening classes or day release. It will also mean that the first requirement is to obtain a post as a trainee DSA. For those following this route the minimum requirement to obtain the Certificate is two years full-time surgery experience plus passing the final examinations and practical tests. The alternative way of qualifying as a DSA is to take a one or two year's full-time course at a dental hospital or FE College. A list of the places which offer such courses comes with the pack from the General Dental Council. These courses will also normally provide the student with practical experience so that they finish the course as fully qualified and are therefore in a good position to apply for jobs.

A DSA has to undertake many different kinds of activities as a part of the job. These can be 'medical' – Assisting with treatment, preparation of filling materials; 'organisational' – Preparing the surgery, arranging appointments, dealing with paperwork; 'personal' – Reassuring anxious patients, comforting crying children. They also have to be able to work closely with a dentist by being able to anticipate the next step in treatment and doing their part in creating a good professional relationship that does not crack under pressure.

As can be imagined the success or otherwise of a dental practice will depend almost as much on the personalities and abilities of the DSAs as the actual dentists. DSAs also work in hospitals, schools, large industrial plants and the armed services. Some eventually move into teaching on training courses. Part-time work is also very often available for qualified DSAs.

Dental Technician

The role of dental technicians can be understood by noting that, apart from fillings, every other treatment that involves placing repair material in the mouth needs the services of a dental technician. This includes crowns, bridges, dentures, orthodontic braces and more complex devices for serious birth defects or facial injuries. The work of a dental technician involves the painstaking application of technical knowledge. They will normally work in a commercial dental laboratory. In 1995 the salaries for qualified technicians ranged from around £12,000 per year to £24,000 per year. The top salaries would only be paid to technicians working in a managerial capacity.

To qualify as a dental technician you have to attend college where success on the course is assessed by academic examinations and practical tests. You also need some work experience. The entry requirement for starting on a course is four GSCEs at grade C or above, of which two should be in science subjects, or a recognised equivalent to these. There are two main routes to qualifying as a dental technician: the first is to obtain a training place at a dental laboratory and attend college on a day release basis. This will take at least five years, but you will of course be paid during that five years. The alternative is to attend a three or four year full-time course at a college or at a NHS hospital or laboratory. These courses will also normally arrange for students to have the necessary work experience. The addresses of relevant colleges and local health authorities are in the General Dental Council's pack. The title of the qualification is the 'National Diploma in Science (Dental Technology)'. Once this diploma is obtained it is then possible to apply for inclusion in the United Kingdom Register of Dental Technicians. For many technicians this first qualification will be the first step and they will undertake further study leading to higher qualifications with consequent further responsibility and pay in laboratories, or alternatively to research work in hospitals.

Unlike dentists and DSAs it is difficult for young people to know what work as a dental technician might involve. If anyone is at all interested it might be well worth their while to visit a dental laboratory. They are listed in yellow pages and you should be able to find one locally that will allow a visit.

Dental Hygienist

Within health care there is a need for people to work at levels just below the professional level of doctor or dentist. A dental hygienist fits into this category. They are qualified to use dental instruments in order to undertake treatment like scaling and polishing, fissure sealing and application of fluorides. For dental hygienists this aspect of treatment is usually in addition to their main role, which is advising and training children and adults on personal oral hygiene. Dental hygienists normally work in large dental practices, hospitals and schools. Very often they will spend their time moving between these areas with particular days or half days in each. In 1995 they were paid on a scale ranging from around £11,000 per year to £15,000 per year.

In order to qualify as a dental hygienist you need to take a one-year full-time course. These courses are offered by almost all the dental hospitals in the UK. The academic entry requirement for these courses is five GSCEs at grade C or above, or another equivalent qualification. Like dentists they also need to be manually dextrous and to be patient and understanding with people of all ages. Becoming a dental hygienist is normally seen as a step up from being a dental surgery assistant, so you would also normally be expected to possess a National Certificate for Dental Surgery Assistants.

The names of those completing the course and passing the examination for the Diploma in Dental Hygiene are then entered in the Roll of Dental Hygienists, maintained by the General Dental Council. Dental Hygienists may not practise in the United Kingdom unless their names are included on that roll.

Dental Therapist

Dental therapists are another category who work just below the professional level of dentists. They are trained to fulfil a 'specialist' role within dental health care. Dental therapists do not generally work in general practice. They work in hospitals or the community service (which includes schools). They advise patients on dental health matters and carry out a wide range of treatments including simple fillings and the extraction of deciduous teeth. They are also qualified to administer local anaesthetics. Another part of the job of a dental therapist can be to provide an education service to schools in which case they also need to have some of the qualities of a teacher. In 1995 the salaries of dental therapists ranged from around £12,000 to £18,000 per year.

At present the only place that offers the two year full time course that leads to qualification as a dental therapist is the Dental Auxiliary School of the London Hospital Medical College. In order to enter this course students have to be at least eighteen years old. They have to have five CSCEs at grade C or an equivalent qualification. The subjects should normally include English and a science. They also need to hold the National Certificate for Dental Surgery Assistants. On successful completion of this course students are entered into the General Dental Council's Roll of Dental Hygienists as well as the Roll of Dental Therapists.

Index